IAN M. FRASER

STRANGE FIRE

First published 1994

ISBN 0 947988 67X

© 1994, Wild Goose Publications / The Iona Community

Wild Goose Publications
Unit 15, Six Harmony Row, Glasgow G51 3BA

Wild Goose Publications is the publishing division
of the Iona Community.

Scottish Charity No. SCO03794. Limited Company Reg. No. SCO96243.

A catalogue record for this book is available from the British Library.

Scriptural quotations bear the author's nuances.

We gratefully acknowledge the contributions of

THE RUSSELL TRUST

and

THE DRUMMOND TRUST
3 PITT TERRACE, STIRLING

towards the publication costs of this book.

Printed in Great Britain by The Cromwell Press, Melksham, Wiltshire

Jesus said, 'I have come to cast fire on the earth and how I long that it be already kindled.' (Luke 12.49)

I walk the earth's thin crust and underneath
fire surges, pressing on my feet,
eager to swallow, whole,
dreams, ventures – o this fragile self
of faith and fear compounded. Nothing done
has a sure outcome. Loser take all.
Feet descend towards the abyss,
fire waits to devour ...

This is the way to live! Life's enterprise
strangled and raped by cossetting
flowers on surprise. Our God contrives
footholds where none are seen; and meets
hesitant steps of faith with ground
conjured from nothing. So our way
is sure only when robbed of evidence.

I walk this day,
like one who walked on waves ...

TO

MARGARET AND MARGOT

SHINING SPIRITS

CONTENTS

The start of their journey together: Margaret and Ian on honeymoon, Iona, 1943.

PREFACE

Margaret started it. A month or two before she died, when there was still no hint of the second cancer which would carry her off so swiftly, she said, 'We could depart this life at any time. We need to get down the stories.' I knew what she meant – stories which formed a kind of heritage of our life together, especially those which had been told by word of mouth only, which might also speak to others. After her death, I started gathering these. When I looked at them carefully I realized that the germs of prayers and hymns were embedded in the narratives. These could be tapped and developed. Here, story and reflection are given on opposite pages. The hymns are in a companion publication, *The Try It Out Hymn Book.*[1]

Although I was the one to be given official assignments, I was conscious of Margaret's being with me even when we were half a world away from one another. Her presence sharpened my vision and strengthened my spirit. It still does after her death. This is our book.

She always had concerns of her own to follow through. In Selly Oak, Birmingham, for instance, she worked in the fields of interfaith dialogue, development education and Tools for Self Reliance. When, with my retirement as Dean in Selly Oak Colleges, I was asked to consider tackling new areas of work, I made a condition. I was no longer prepared to undertake solo what Margaret might be prepared to do with me in direct partnership.

It was then that the British Missionary Societies and Boards proposed a joint five-year assignment which delighted our hearts. We were asked to get a Third World perspective on basic Christian communities – small cells of people seeking a true understanding of the Christian faith by living it imaginatively; then visit or revisit b.c.c.s in Europe, East and West; and bring back insights for the renewal of the Church in Britain.

During our travels, we took notes separately and compared them only at the end. The different emphases and angles of vision resulted in a three-dimensional frame for stories drawn from shared experiences.

The book is dedicated to her, and with her, to Margot McWilliam who lives with her beyond death. Margot and her husband, Stuart, have been lifelong friends of ours.

1. For details, please send an s.a.e. to The Try it Out Hymn Book, The Iona Community, Pearce Institute, 840 Govan Road, Glasgow G51 3UU.

GOD WITH US AND BEYOND US

SAN MIGUELITO, PANAMA, EARLY 1970S

One night, when a planned engagement fell through, I wandered among the homes of the community. There I met a man I had previously talked to while he was washing down a car. Nine months before, Bill had been a hopeless drunk. Now he lived by doing odd jobs. I asked if there was anything happening which would be interesting for me to go to in the area. He said he was a lay pastor and was just about to conduct a liturgy of the Word, and that I was very welcome to come along.

The bare house in which the people gathered was really one small room with two partitions breaking it up. For a good part of the service, two of the children of the household were crying intermittently; occasionally one would get up to pull back the curtain of one of the partitions and gaze at us. Outside the dogs barked and howled, competing with a transistor radio. On the kitchen table was a cross with a lighted candle on either side. Over his open-necked shirt Bill placed a stole and was ready to start. About ten neighbours, most in their early twenties or thirties, pressed in, some bringing their own chairs or stools with them. I shared a tatty couch with an older man.

There was an introductory section in which people sang and gave responses. Then a passage from the Acts of the Apostles, used throughout the parish that week, was taken for study. Practically everyone participated in building up an understanding of the passage. At one point Bill was pushing them too strongly in emphasizing God's presence in the midst of life. They would not have this. 'We know God is in the thick of things where we are,' they said. 'We believe that. But that is not all. God is also beyond us. We do not know how God can be with us and beyond us. But that's just the way it is.'

After about forty minutes of Bible study, those who took part were asked to offer prayers and all but two responded. Another song was sung, there were one or two more responses, and the service ended.

* * *

REFLECTION

God the Father, you created and go on creating. Your will is to release the creativity in human beings, all made in your likeness. You call us to throw our lives on the scales for a new world. We praise and bless you who have trusted us with life, well knowing the risks you ran.

God the Son, who laid aside your glory that you might become one with us, and died that you might overcome death and secure life abundant for your human family, you stand witness to a true Way for folk to take. We praise and bless you that we may live as those who are heirs to all the promises.

God the Holy Spirit, who brings home to us all that the Father designed and that the Son accomplished – you dwell in us, you renew us, you inspire us, you open up new paths for our feet. We praise and bless you that you conspire with us to change the earth into the world of God's promise.

In our day, Father, Son and Holy Spirit, you do new things. We bless you that what many prophets and righteous people longed to see and hear in their time and did not, we see and hear in our time. The poor are lifted high. The despised and rejected preach and prophesy. The discarded point the important to true ways of life. Gifts are distributed among the whole human family, including the least likely. This is your doing and it is marvellous in our eyes.

PRAYER

Strengthen the foolish and weak things of this world that they may confound those that are mighty. Strengthen those who, having been downgraded by others, testify with convincing power that you are making all things new.

Strengthen those in positions of power and authority who may feel threatened by this Church 'born from below', that they may not quench the Spirit but be themselves open to transformation.

And, Lord, look into my own heart to sift and strengthen me:

– forgive my instinctive despising and shunning of people such as ....

– forgive my playing safe when risks of faith are called for, such as ....

– forgive my unreadiness to offer my body, my being, as a living sacrifice;

– forgive me for being deaf to unwelcome voices, blind to unwelcome sights;

– have mercy on me who thus betrays my baptism and my calling.

Lord, I believe, help my unbelief.

Amen.

The Wise Men came from quite outwith the Hebrew/Christian tradition and yet they helped to shape it and became part of it.

The following experiences came to me from completely out of the blue. When, I was working as Dean at Selly Oak Colleges, and reaching the standard age of retirement, I was invited to stay on. But a dean can put too personal a stamp on a new department which he has helped bring into being so my wife, Margaret, and I decided to go. It meant facing a void. We had no place, no house, no function to fulfil. We wondered whether that was where a line was to be drawn to end our main life-work.

It was then there came a knock at the door. A gypsy stood there with her basket of wares. I recollect the intent look in her eyes. She shielded them with her hand, scrutinized me, and said, 'You are a loving man and greatly loved. Your relationship with your wife is something special. You have a wide range of friends rather than a few close ones. You are wondering what lies ahead. I can tell you that there's a big task still waiting for you. Do you want any clothes-pegs, pan-scourers, cotton reels?' When I said that I had no need of any of these, she went away content as if that had not been the main point of her visit.

A few months later, the British Missionary Societies and Boards asked Margaret and myself to undertake a five-year joint assignment on the significance of basic Christian communities for the renewal of British Churches; I was asked to act, concurrently, as research-consultant to the Scottish Churches' Council.

The incident with the gypsy took me back to 1942. I was a labour-industrial chaplain in industry. One Sunday I was passing the time of day with a few other young folk when they decided to visit someone they knew. When we got there, I found they were having their palms read and I decided to join in although it wasn't my sort of thing.

My turn came. The fortune teller examined the lines, appeared startled, and looked more carefully: 'Your field is going to be the world,' she concluded. I could get nothing more out of her. How could she have foreseen, at the beginning, that different assignments would eventually take me to eighty-seven countries?

By that year, 1942, I was already trained and licensed to preach and had two degrees. But I had walked an irregular path and ordination was delayed until 1946. When it came, the service could scarcely have been more pedestrian. I kept assuring myself that what mattered was the affirmation of the Church. That was where reality lay, and not in my sense of anticlimax. Hands were laid on me. What followed could be likened to nothing I have read about except Jesus' baptism. The heavens opened. From beyond all time and space came a thunderbolt that lodged in my being. My emotional temperature did not rise a fraction. But from that point on I knew I was claimed.

* * *

The day I was born was the day I was born:
one red life from another torn.

The day I was born was the day of God's claim:
I, who'd been named, was given a name.

The day I was born was the day I was wed:
life knit with life spelled life from the dead.

Under the Trinity, a trinity sends
through time and space to Kingdom ends.

Have you ever found that God responds to straight, rough theological talk and despises the polished language of deference?

When working for the World Council of Churches 'Participation in Change' programme, I took a plane from Barquisimeto, Venezuela, to Caracas. My intention was to make contact with the shanty dwellers in the hills, to find out how they coped with change when they moved from rural areas into the city and found no place to stay.

I had tried as usual to get some introduction to a contact person or family beforehand, totally without success. As I got on the plane I took God to task: 'Look, a covenant's a covenant. I've done all I can as far as I can make out. You have your side to see to so please get off your butt and make sure that this is not a fruitless journey – unless you have another plan up your sleeve.'

The pilot of the plane made his ascent at a very steep angle. When the plane straightened out, a young lady came up to me. She held in her hand a plastic folder which I had placed on the empty seat beside me. 'I think this is yours,' she said. I was not even aware that it had slipped through the back of the seat and slid down to rest at her feet.

'I was looking for an excuse to speak to you in any case,' she told me, so I invited her to sit in the vacant seat beside me. 'I just wanted to ask,' she said, 'whether you work for the World Council of Churches from their headquarters in Geneva. That is where I picture you.' 'Did we serve together in some commission or committee?' I asked, puzzled, but ready to believe that I had quite forgotten some occasion of collaboration. 'No it wasn't that,' she said. 'It was simply that, some months ago, I was shown over the headquarters of the WCC in Geneva, and I think I remember noticing you there. When you got on the plane I thought I remembered you.'

'And what is your work in Caracas?' I asked, in due course. 'I am the liaison worker between the City Council and the slum-dwellers in the hills around,' she replied.

* * *

REFLECTION

God is to be rollicked with, as with a child or a puppy.

God is to be looked at with silent awe while we suck the thumb of contemplation before such majesty and love.

God is to be screamed at for failing us.

God is to be accepted with the furniture.

God is always to be there to deal with bruises and tears.

God is to be obeyed, sometimes reluctantly, sometimes joyfully.

God is to be taken by the throat, shaken, and given no peace until something gives.

God is to be trusted when we jump.

God is to be run to in whatever clothes we stand up in.

God is to be spoken to in our own natural speech.

God is to be twinkled back at.

God is to be rested in, held snug and tight.

God is to be allowed to enrich and enlarge the divine life at the fount of ours.

We need the heart of a child to respond truly to God.

TRUSTING GOD

To love means at times to let go, putting a shield of prayer around the loved one.

In 1972, Pastor Ayadji – a member of the Apostolic Action Team working in the Fon area of Dahomey (later to be called Benin) – had a difficult choice to make when he became a Christian. He was part of a community whose religion was animist and who set great store by respect paid to ancestors and on rites fulfilled to acknowledge their presence and authority. He could have gone elsewhere and he believed his people would have welcomed such a choice because it would have got rid of the embarrassment of a member of their community belonging to another faith. But if he had done so, there would have been no Christian witness in their midst, and to that he felt called from the beginning of his new life. He knew that if he stayed there would be attempts to poison him since he would be thought of as a cancerous growth in the body of the community which would infect the whole if it were not got rid of.

If he stayed he would be expected to take part in ancestor rites. However, he felt he could do this for he believed in the Communion of Saints and life beyond death so the two lines of belief did not seem too far apart. Ancestors were not perceived to be gods but superhuman beings who needed to be kept informed and consulted about every development in the community's life. He decided to stay. He offered sacrifices to the ancestors. He kept vigilant in case of poisoning attempts.

A harder decision awaited him. His young son was chosen by the community to be trained in the beliefs and uses of fetishes. If the father refused, the boy would become an object of resentment, and his father feared that because of his youth he would be less alert to poisoning attempts. Pastor Ayadji told himself, 'If the power of God has shielded me in all my life in this community, will it not also shield my son?' He let him go.

And so the pastor won respect and understanding for a faith which must have seemed at first to be one which would threaten to cut an African community from its own indigenous roots and its own valued practices.

* * *

REFLECTION

'We can learn from animists. We have too few names for God to convey the immense variety of ways in which God meets with human beings and makes himself known.' (Bishop Adegbola at the Central Committee of the WCC, Enugu)

PRAYER

Lord God, in whom we live and move and have our being, we meet you everywhere, on hills and in slums, in excitements and in routines, in the good and in the bad parts of life. In everything and everyone you are waiting to be known. We bless you that you are no strange god but the God of love and judgement made known in Jesus Christ. Make us alert to see you at every turn of the road, in every situation, in every human encounter, recognizing your touch which gives people and places significance.

Lord God, we bless you that we live and move in families. We bless you for the ties of blood and kinship which bind us in one bundle of life and which nourish our own lives with a special kind of sustaining love. Make us ready, when we have to go separate ways, to put a shield of prayer about one another, confident in your ability to hold and keep us whatever we have to face and wherever we go.

Lord God, in whom we live and move and have our being, we bless you that we live and move in a great company of those whom death does not divide from us. They rejoice to see you face to face. They give us heart for life's battles. We are one great community, the communion of saints; we are at one with all kinds of ordinary folk whose lives are capped and crowned beyond death. Make us aware that you and they are companioning our road when the struggles get hard and when we need to think twice about the way to take.

All this we ask in the name of Jesus Christ
Amen.

'HELP MY UNBELIEF'

In the 1950s, when I had just become Parish Minister of Rosyth, and was visiting people in one area, I went to a door, and when it was opened I recognized the secretary of the local Communist Party.

He said to me, roughly, 'What are you doing at my door? I'm not one of your lot.' I said that I had been appointed to serve the whole parish not just a congregation, and, since he was in the parish, I was visiting him as I visited others. He looked at me darkly as if my visit were an intrusion. I went on, 'You can shut the door in my face if you want to. What you can't do is prevent my knocking on it.' Reluctantly, maybe conceding that I had a point, he talked to me for a few minutes and then indicated that that was enough personal contact as far as he was concerned.

The area took a long time to visit and I went back some weeks later for a second time. He seemed to have softened a bit and was ready to talk with me about justice and injustice in the area. The third time occurred when neighbours told me that he wanted desperately to see me. He grabbed me and pulled me inside. His wife was in hospital. He loved her deeply and was very concerned. He went into detail of how the trouble had developed, and how she was. At the end, he asked if I would pray for his wife and himself, there and then.

I replied that we had begun to respect one another and to understand one another. There was no need for him to 'act religious'. He should feel free to keep the integrity of his own genuine position. His response was immediate: 'Nane o' yer bloody nonsense. Get doon on yer knees wi' me and pray for my wife and mysel'.'

So I got down on my knees with the secretary of the Communist Party in Rosyth and we held up in prayer the woman he loved to the God in whom he did not believe.

* * *

PRAYER

Lord God, you search our hearts. You know what is deep in us. You know where we really stand.

We praise and bless you that you are not taken in by appearances, by professions of faith which find poor expression in the way we live our daily lives, by professions of unfaith which actual actions contradict;
– and confess to you the fear in our hearts that you who see through us cannot abide the half-hearted way in which our public lives testify to you.

We praise and bless you that you stay with those who are put off by our language and habits and unpreparedness to stand up and be counted on the side of justice;
– and confess to you the fear in our hearts that we who are called to reveal you to the nations have hidden your true face from them.

We praise and bless you that you accept people as they are, in love for the world to which Christ came; and look to all kinds of people to respond to you in their own time and manner;
– and confess to you the fear in our hearts that we bring shame upon you, by our conduct towards some people, declaring them to be unacceptable, cutting them off as if that were your verdict upon them.

We praise and bless you for the integrity which marks the lives of so many women, men and children who may not be aware that they are living to your glory;
– and tell you of the joy in our hearts that, above and beyond everything we do which might obscure your face, you keep faith with people who do not know your name and you honour their straight and honest ways.

Look in mercy on us, Lord. We have no excuses. We have nothing to turn to, nothing to hold on to but that love in Jesus Christ which forgives and restores. Grant us new opportunity, by amendment of life, to testify to your transforming presence in the world.

In the name of the Father, the Son and the Holy Spirit

Amen.

'I CALL YOU FRIENDS'

In Jerusalem, I was looking for the Patriarch Vicar of the Greek Catholic Church, Archbishop Laham. I saw a gate with a cross on it. A ruddy-faced, bearded Orthodox ecclesiastic answered my knock and motioned me inside. When he heard I was Scottish he danced for joy, his eyes twinkled, and he gave me a great bear-hug and kiss. At times, thereafter, he would say 'Scottish' with great delight and give me another bear-hug and kiss. Clearly you don't need heavenly visitors if earthly ones come from the right part of the world.

He showed me round his small icon-clad church. He then offered me a selection of liqueurs and my choice of ouzo confirmed my status in his eyes. We sat and enjoyed one another's company. To accompany the ouzo, he produced delicious honey pastries. Occasionally we tried a little conversation, seeking to make up by gestures what was lacking in words.

'How often do you have a service in the day?' I asked salting my talk with some words of classical Greek and pointing at my watch. 'From Athena,' he said contentedly, pointing at himself. 'Are you a monk or a priest – are you married?' I asked. 'From Athena,' he answered. 'Are there others who officiate with you?' I enquired. 'From Athena,' he replied, contentedly.

Ours was a perfectly rational and satisfying form of communication. For we did not depend on words. I was reminded of my greeting to Jim Wallis of the Soujourners Community in the States: 'We've known one another for so long it is high time we met!' There is a communion of saints in heaven and on earth. On rare occasions you recognize strangers and feel you have known them all your life.

When we parted, my new blood-brother took me to the gate and pointed me in the wrong direction. How could he have been expected to know, as a Greek Orthodox, where the Greek Catholic patriarchy was? After all, it was a good fifty yards from his own building.

* * *

Jesus said, 'No longer do I call you servants, for a servant does not know what his master is about. I have called you friends, because I have made known to you everything that I heard from my Father.' (John 15.15)

PRAYER

Almighty God, God of power and might, father and mother of us all – like a lion springing from deep grasses you take us by surprise. When we are at your mercy and terrified, we find that you croon over us like a lioness over her cubs and lick us into shape. We rejoice in your friendship and all friendships which flow from it. We rejoice that we can be at ease with you who are the Most High; that you give us space, not appearing in majesty to subdue us but remaining invisible – that we might, in our own time and way, respond to your friendship. We give thanks for .... and .... in whose presence we can relax and be refreshed.

We rejoice that you accept us exactly as we are, not holding our deficiencies against us, yet by your very presence making us more aware of them and more determined to overcome them; and that thus we are allowed to grow as ourselves, and make our own choices, so that our lives are shaped and reshaped with our own agreement. We give thanks for .... and .... who free us to be ourselves.

We rejoice that we do not need words all the time; that together we can kindle friendship with one another, rest in one another, feel intoxicated as lovers, or content just to be in the other's presence; and we give thanks for .... and .... with whom we can enjoy the gift of shared silence.

We rejoice that it is not just at the high and low points of life that you are with us; but that, unseen, you rub shoulders with us in our routines, that you are ready to pass the time of day with us as well as deal with serious matters, and that you also stand aside and leave us alone to get on with it. We give thanks for our neighbours – for .... and .... whose laughter and banter can lighten the day.

It takes our breath away, you, the Most High are our friend and put friends in our way along life's path! Alleluia!

Amen.

GOD'S ARTISTRY

Mesquite trees are cursed for their thorns which tear clothes and flesh. But in drought they blessedly harbour water. They also produce nourishing pods. These factors have saved the lives of many a Comanche and Sioux hunted by the US army.

In the early 1970s, as one of the staff of a Unit of the World Council of Churches in Geneva, I spent a day with artists who worked with paint, wood and stone – to listen to them, and to see what they were making of life and find out how they expressed their insights.

At one point an Amerindian artist put a wood carving in my hand and asked, 'What does that say to you?' 'It speaks of the kind of person in the light of whom my life will be judged,' I replied. 'Say more,' he urged. 'The figure is one of great dignity accompanied by humility and poverty,' I replied. 'The face, which could be that of a man or a woman has either not yet come fully into being or has been half rubbed out. The sculpture speaks of people the world over who are made in the image of God, who have their identity as children of God denied or eroded – but who, in spite of all, still carry about with them the signs of their Godgiven worth. If the life I live relates effectively to such people, if it gives them their place and respects their lives and their voices, then it may be acceptable to God. If it doesn't, it won't be.'

The artist had already told me that he 'found it in the wood' of a Mesquite tree. He had not used any colouring – the brown of the human being and the creamy brown of the garment had been 'waiting in the wood', ready for him to disclose it in its completeness. 'When I found it in the wood,' he said, 'I knew it had to live with someone. I have been waiting to be told who that was. You are the "someone". If you are prepared to accept it, you must promise me two things. You will not offer me money for it. If it stops speaking to you and you stop living with it, you must search till you find someone to whom it will speak, with whom it will live, and hand it over.'

I have never stopped living with it. It has never stopped speaking to me. It helps to anchor me in fundamentals.

* * *

PRAYER

God the Lord, how marvellously you have fashioned the world and all its creatures – wild things on the hills and animals around our doors, a myriad of wings against the sky; the teeming world of insects, sea creatures, great and small; sky and clouds, mountains and valleys, mighty waters.

– And how fearsomely we have re-fashioned it, in cruelty to creatures given to share the earth with us, and in the plundering of nature.

God the Lord, how marvellously you have fashioned folk, all made in your likeness, endowing us with abilities to respond to your giving through many skills with wood and stone, metal and paint, with graceful bodily movement, with evocative sound, and with skills in rearing families and managing life in general.

– And how fearsomely we have re-fashioned it, turning to evil ends what you gave to enrich human life.

We bless you that so many perceptive people faithfully throw light on our human condition forcing us to face up to what we have made of life, raising our eyes and spirits to discern what life could hold for the whole human family and for all creatures.

We bless you for

– artists and designers, architects and writers;

– dancers and fashion models and athletes;

– bands and groups and orchestras;

– parents and foster homes and social workers;

– shop stewards, personnel managers and deans;

– neighbours and community councils and teachers.

Open our eyes to the world as you have fashioned it to be.

Open our ears to the world's cries of sorrow and joy.

Open our nostrils to the corrupting smell of oppression and the fragrance of wholesome living.

Give us a sure touch to craft our own life so that it is a glory to you and a blessing to humankind and thus to the whole Creation.

In Jesus' name
Amen.

Over the generations, a fishing community had won a living from Lake Laguna in the northern part of the Philippines. During the dictatorship of Ferdinand Marcos, capitalists began to make inroads, establishing fish farms without any legitimate basis for their action. The fishing community sent protests to the President. They were ignored. A social worker told me how she had come to their aid.

First she encouraged them to develop a campaign of letter-writing. One day two large sacks of protest mail were placed on Marcos' desk. What had once been an irritation had clearly become a running sore. He appointed a committee of investigation to deal with the fishing folk. He made sure that it was filled with technical and legal experts who could be trusted to outmanoeuvre and silence the protesters.

The Laguna people were fearful at the news. But the social worker gathered the representatives of the people together to look at the total task of investigation of written deeds, of rights which had traditional but not written acknowledgement, and at the law of the land where it was relevant to their case. They divided up the work, giving small portions of it to different members, who, when they had completed their piece of research, remitted it to the person who was to represent them at the meeting with the government committee. When the committee of investigation arrived, confident of winning their case, the fisherfolk wiped the floor with them.

When the conquistadors settled in Guatemala they staked out the 'unclaimed land', powerful leaders dividing it between themselves. The Indians stood amazed at such foolishness. Anyone with sense must surely realize that land is not there to be owned but to be related to. It is for all to use in due proportion, animal and human being alike. They made a joke of it at first. With their hands they shaped imaginary bundles of air and faced up to one another, saying, 'This is my portion of air, not yours. Don't try to get your hands on it.' Then they fell about laughing at the foolishness of the foreigners.

* * *

REFLECTION

Let us rejoice in water, land and air as incredible inventions of God.

Let us give thanks for water which refreshes us and sustains us; which soothes tired feet and relieves aching limbs; which delights the eye in waterfall and fountain; which nourishes crops on land and supplies food in river and sea; in which we can swim, surf and sail;

– which in its own right can destroy in storm and flood, and by our selfishness and carelessness can destroy through exploitation and pollution;

– that we may learn to cherish the gift and share it with all human and other living creatures as something we do not own but are called to apportion fairly and use joyfully; and may those who would exploit it for gain and rob others of its use be made sensitive to God's will.

Let us give thanks for land firm beneath feet; revelling in its capacity to produce and nourish grasses and flowers and vegetables and trees; land preserving hidden treasures of the past and material resources for the present; turned over by the plough and sweet in the morning air; land providing rooting for nations and cultures and families;

– which in its own right can destroy in earthquake and eruption, and by our selfishness and carelessness can be made barren;

– that we may learn to cherish the gift and share it with all human and other living creatures as something we do not own but are called to apportion fairly and use joyfully; and that those who would exploit it for gain and rob others of its use may be made sensitive to God's will.

Let us give thanks for air caressing cheeks, gambolling over hill and plain; refreshing the morning and unburdening the tiredness of evening; bringing hope to trapped miners; sustaining airmen and birds in flight; relieving the asthmatic and enhancing the prowess of the athlete; air, symbol of the Holy Spirit;

– which in its own right can destroy in tornado and hurricane, and by our selfishness and carelessness can poison through pollution;

– that we may learn to cherish the gift and secure its quality for all human and other living creatures to God's glory and the blessing of the whole Creation.

THE WORLD: GIVEN FOR ALL TO ENJOY (2)

INTERVIEW IN A 'SAFE HOUSE', THE PHILIPPINES, 1973, WITH
ED DE LA TORRE – A FILIPINO THEOLOGIAN HUNTED BY MARCOS
FOR SIDING WITH THE POOR.

On one particular occasion, a group of farmers in Pampanga who had been tenants for maybe three generations, felt the need to consult the priest. They knew that they should own the land, and that their feeling was right – it was not avarice or greed which motivated them. But they wanted to be told it was right; they had been told for so long to stay quiet and docile.

So they talked with this priest: 'Look, we feel this land is ours, but don't have a law that tells us it's ours. Nor have we learned in our catechism or in your sermons that it's ours. So would you please dig into your Bible and theology, and tell us where it says it is right that we should own this land?' Well that priest – he's dead now – eventually answered: 'The only thing I can remember is in the Ten Commandments, the ninth or the tenth, "Thou shall not covet thy neighbour's goods".'

It was at this point, I'd say, that theology came in, but not in any familiar terms. They came up with a very beautiful analogy, very sexual because that's close to the language of the peasant. A young man goes to a province and sees a beautiful girl. He marries her, in fact he gets a 'title' to her, a marriage contract. But he doesn't consummate the marriage. He goes to other places and he takes other lovers.

Then it happens that somebody else comes along and sees her. She is alone, she is lonely, she is desirable; and so he lives with her, and supports her, and they bear children. After many years, the legal husband comes back and sees this other man shacked up with his legal wife. He says, 'Hey, that's my wife, I have the title to her, here is the document.' The farmers then asked, 'Look, who is the real husband? Is it the one who is sleeping with her, who has children with her, who lives with her, who loves her? They are married to each other in the deepest sense of the word. Most people would agree with that. Yes, but apply it to the land and they will call you a Communist! Can you get any priest to tell you that it is right to own the land just because you are the one who is wed to it?'

* * *

REFLECTION

If the earth is the Lord's and the fullness thereof; if we are to manage it as trustees to fulfil God's purpose for it; all forms of ownership are thus relativized. No person, no nation has a final right to land.

The warning is given in Leviticus 25.23: 'No land shall be sold in perpetuity, because the land belongs to me and you are my lodgers and tenants.' Where accumulation takes place, others are robbed of their share of God's provision: 'Woe to those who add house to house and join field to field till everyone else is deprived.' (Isaiah 5.8). The Jubilee enactments in the Old Testament were designed to return alienated land to the original owners.

For people and for nations, land ownership can take on an idolatrous aspect, being used to justify personal acquisitions of property and excuse a nation's 'historical destiny'. Amos puts this latter aspect into proportion, putting all nations on the same footing before God. 'Are you not as the Cushites to me, o sons of Israel? declares the Lord. Have I not brought up Israel from the land of Egypt – and the Philistines from Caphtar and the Aramaeans from Kir?' (Amos 9.7)

Is any theological problem more pressing today than ownership and use of land?

PRAYER

Lord God

In you alone is our security. Our worth comes from being made in your image and in being loved with an everlasting love:

– not from historical achievements;

– not from ownership to which others may acknowledge our title;

– not from seeking status over other people or other nations.

We pray for people and nations who seek to validate their significance through possession of large or richly endowed territories; for those deprived of the land they need to sustain their families; for those who make land fertile, and then have it taken away by the powerful; for indigenous people whose land is invaded, polluted, destroyed; for all exploited people who work the land and are denied the rewards.

Enable us to seek your Kingdom of righteousness tenaciously.

In Jesus Christ's name we ask this.

Amen.

Wherever I went in the world on World Council of Churches business, I took the chance not just to produce interviews and reports but to 'feel the life' of communities (in the good Quaker phrase).

One night in Port au Prince, Haiti, I was the only white person wandering among the people. Folk had spilled out from their crowded homes, making the street their meeting place. They conversed, played board games which were unfamiliar to me. A quarrel flared up between two women. They flew at one another. Before neighbours could separate them, one had ripped the other's blouse down the front disclosing her breasts. Then life settled back.

On two occasions during my return journey, women came up behind me, took hold of my hand and offered themselves. One was black but not Negroid, clearly of mixed race; the other brown. Both had fine figures. They walked with lithe, graceful movements. When their offer was refused they did not persist but moved quietly away. What straits people must find themselves in who offer their lovely bodies for a pittance. The price? In each case, the equivalent of 40p for the night – the price of survival.

My daughter Anne and her husband had taken us from their home in Vientiane to Chiang Mai for a holiday break. Before settling for the night, I had gone down to the front of the hotel for a breath of fresh air. A bicycle-rickshaw man spotted me, moved forward: 'I got number one girl in Thailand for you: $10 for the night.' A colleague saw his chance: 'I got number one girl in Thailand for you: $5 for the night.' I said, 'I got number one girl in Thailand waiting for me in my bedroom.' They moved away disappointed. I was not telling fibs. Wherever Margaret went with me in my travels, she was to me number one girl in the country in which we were staying.

On only one other occasion in my life have I seen someone as broken up inside as the Taiwanese man who had just come off the plane from Tokyo. Sitting near him had been a company of Japanese men. A tour conductor had moved between the rows taking orders just as a waiter might: tall or short, fat or thin, one-night stands or the same woman for the whole time ....

On their arrival in Taipei living human flesh would be available to fit the menu choices. It was my first direct encounter with sex-tourism.

* * *

REFLECTION

Remember:

– *parents so poor in many parts of the world, that they will sell children not yet in their teens into prostitution to provide for the rest of the family and to supply themselves with drugs;*

– *women who would not survive if they did not ply the trade;*

– *women raped, penetrated to the inmost citadel of their being, so defiled that they wonder if they will ever get charge of their bodies and lives again;*

– *women all made in the image of God, treated merely as usables and discardables.*

Consider our share in this:

– *if we do not fight for a fairer distribution of earth's resources, so that pressure on parents is lifted;*

– *if we do not fight for a fairer deal for women and a truer relationship between the sexes;*

– *if we do not combat systems exploitive of human relationships.*

Remember:

– *according to biblical insights sexual intercourse was given to be a kind of 'knowing' not a selfish and perfunctory using;*

– *the domination of men over women is a sign of fallen humanity (note Genesis ch. 3).*

PRAYER

God the Lord, help your human family to honour you with their bodies.

At San Martin, near Barcelona, people from basic Christian communities asked me about Selly Oak, Birmingham. I told them of the nearness of Longbridge, the Austin Motors works down the road. They were immediately interested and asked me when there was a dispute at that works how the churches in that locality reacted. Did they mainly take the side of the workforce or of the management? I had to confess that they took very little direct interest as congregations in any industrial dispute.

'Oh, come on,' they said, 'We know that there will be different reactions in different circumstances. Most times we need to side with the workforce. When there is a dispute there is usually some real injustice at the root of it and the workforce are those who take the brunt. There are times when we should side with the management because they seem to have a point which the workforce are a bit blind to. In each case, one of our jobs, as Christians, is to keep the one side open to the other. If you take the side of the shop-floor workers, your identification with them includes the business of communicating to them something which belongs to the management's view of things. If you believe that the management are in the right, you encourage them to appreciate how the shop-floor workers are placed, and how they are reacting. But you always need to take sides and not sit on the fence.

'Of course, there has to be a good foundation from which to act. You have to build up an understanding of the development of industry in your area over a period of many years. It takes time and energy. All that we are asking is whether the Churches in the area of Longbridge, usually come out on the side of the workforce or of the management.'

I had to repeat my point about the Church's indifference.

They shook their heads, incredulous. 'How can people claim to be Christians and stay out of such things?' they asked.

* * *

PRAYER

Let us pray for the Churches' industrial mission, putting ourselves in the position of those engaged in industry.

> *Bent to the lot our crafts assign*
> *swayed by deep tides of need and fear*
> *in loyalties torn, the truth unclear*
> *how may we build to your design?*
> *You are the workmen, Lord, not we*
> *all worlds were made at your command*
> *Christ, their sustainer, bared his hand*
> *rescued them from futility*
> *Our part to do what he'll commit*
> *who strides the world and calls folk all*
> *partners in pain and carnival*
> *to grasp the hope he won for it.*

Let us give thanks that industry is no longer treated as alien territory

– that the Church is more aware of large forces at work there, shaping life for good and ill, and recognizes claims other than those of merely personal morality;

– that the idolatrous role of principalities and powers which seek to get life to run their way, not God's, is more clearly understood;

– that the positive contribution of industrial work to the whole of life is better appreciated;

– that concern for the environment and for ethical investment are now on industry's agenda.

Let us pray for industrial chaplains

– in their prayer life and use of biblical insights;

– in their dilemmas, as technically unskilled people seeking to appreciate the stances of people with a great variety of skills;

– in resisting the softening-up which may accompany boardroom hospitality and the temptation to side with over-quick judgements of shop-floor workers;

– in knowing when and how to take sides for righteousness sake or take a middle course for righteousness sake.

Lord God, You require us to replenish and subdue, to tend and keep this earth. May industry's enterprise be marked by the grace and efficiency of your large enterprise for Creation

Amen.

The need for religious faith often goes deep among those who turn their backs on a way of life which has let them down. Writing in 1974 from Six Nations in Grand River Lands in Canada, an Iroquois told me in a letter:

'There are some of us here at Six Nations who are willing to try to rebuild our tattered culture and exist independent from the spiritually dead white society.' They acknowledge: 'We are all amateurs at the task of rebuilding a nation and a culture. The Jews are also trying to do something like this, I suppose. We have some problems in common with them.

'For example, we ask ourselves "what is a Jew?" "what is an Indian?" and neither definition can be made without reference to religion.' Dignity, community, roots are basic elements in the search: 'We would begin taking in our "grandmothers" and "grandfathers" as soon as we began to function. Perhaps the unwanted children also. They would have their sense of belonging restored to them.'

The Indians within this movement are turning their backs on the white man's ways and the white man's God who has not stretched out a hand to help, and going back to the Long House religion of their ancestors. What else is there to do if Christianity has proved to be simply part of an oppressive system?

Another Amerindian has written to me, expressing his anger: 'To us, Hitler killing six million people was not the world-shaking event it was to Europe, from our vantage point of having over forty million indigenous people killed by Europeans, of having whole nations of Indians completely destroyed.'

* * *

PRAYER

Lord God Almighty,

who, in Jesus Christ, showed us a new and living way and taught us to love one another as we have been loved, look with mercy on your world which has learned so little from your mission to it and has caught so little of your Spirit.

We remember the Holocaust, the pitiless destruction of millions of Jewish women, men and children, gypsies, lesbian and gay people and disabled people; the willingness of the destroyers to believe that a race of humankind has an inbuilt vileness and, accordingly, merits elimination;

– and pray that the memory may issue not in vengefulness and injustice-in-reverse, but have a positive, creative effect, producing a more realistic awareness of the depth to which all human nature can fall.

We remember that Jews and Arabs, fellow-Semites, lived in community with one another in many parts of the world for generations, honouring and respecting their differences, appreciating what they hold in common;

– and pray that they may re-establish community where it has been disrupted and learn afresh to live at peace, in justice.

We remember native Indians, their land intruded on, whole nations wiped out, their customs and cultures devalued and destroyed;

– and pray for international action to protect and cherish these ravaged cultures, and to honour their gentle relationship to the world around.

We remember birds, animals and sea-creatures threatened by our activities;

– and pray for a greater awareness of all living things as fellow sharers of this planet, with their own proper rights to be respected.

Lord God, who has made the world so marvellous, with living things swarming over the earth and human beings put in charge,

– help us to manage our relationships with each other in all our different cultures, and with other living creatures, that we lay aside destructive ways. Prepare us for the promised time when war and torture cease, when the wolf shall live with the lamb, and the leopard with the kid, and they shall not hurt and destroy on all your holy mountain. For then the earth will be full of the knowledge of you as the waters cover the sea.

Amen.

In January 1990, representatives of 6,000 small Hungarian Christian communities, now free to meet openly, gathered together to consider responsibilities denied expression under Communism. It was clear to them that to grow into the fullness of faith, prayer and Bible study insights had now to find outlet in social and political commitments.

They looked at the possibility of forming a political party. 'We could call on 100,000 people. No party would have as strong a base as we could muster.' However, they concluded that Christians should not form parties but invest in whatever parties seemed most likely to have priorities not too distant from those of the Kingdom of God.

They asked themselves whether they should support any particular party. The president of the Christian Democrats was present and he argued that his party was the only one based on Christian principles, which walked hand in hand with the Church. (My interpreter stepped aside from her task sufficiently to whisper to me, 'You can imagine with how big a pinch of salt we take that.') The representatives decided that they should not support any *one* party. With integrity Christians had made different political choices and they must be free to continue to do so.

The rest of the day was taken up with the search to find a positive way forward. Clear decisions were agreed:

– members should support whichever parties and pressure groups seemed to have programmes nearest to the concerns of the Kingdom;

– they should encourage those among their community who wanted to stand as candidates for regional and national government to do so, whichever party these supported;

– all should submit their social and political choices and their reasons for these to their own small groups; hear and attend to critical assessments of their actions; and decide in the light of these whether to change course or continue as before.

At the end of the day, my interpreter apologized: 'For decades we have had no opportunity to exercise political responsibilities. You must excuses our immaturity.' Would that we were as mature as they!

* * *

REFLECTION

In his introduction to a selection of Tennyson's poems (Phoenix, 1946), W.H. Auden reflects on the problems encountered by the lyric poet when the muse has deserted him and concludes that Tennyson did not have the wit to do anything other than go on writing. He observes: '... trash is the inevitable result whenever a person tries to do for himself or for others by the writing of poetry what can only be done in some other way, by action, or study or prayer.'

SELF-EXAMINATION

Do I use the range of means open to me to respond to God?

Am I content merely to pray that injustices be remedied – when letters to the press, bombarding M.P.s, protest marches, law courts, civil disobedience provide means of bringing pressure to bear?

Is my action determined by and backed up by study and prayer?

Is it exposed to the critical judgement of fellow Christians?

Poets, thought Wittgenstein, interpret the secrets of the universe. Have I been too busy to attempt to set down what I make of life, even if it be simply for my own clarification of what counts most?

PRAYER

God the Lord,

Forgive the people who call you by your name

– when they take easy ways out and fail to offer the particular kind of obedience which a situation calls for;

– when they make easy judgements, not backed up by adequate homework on realities which have to be faced and on the revelation of your mind;

– when they fail to 'take it to the Church' to get the critical judgement of other Christians on choices they make.

May we put on the whole armour of God for the fight against principalities and powers and spiritual wickedness in high places.

In Jesus Christ's name we ask it

Amen.

TOUGH ASSIGNMENT

During the severe droughts which took place in the early 1960s, the National Christian Council of Kenya stretched a helping hand to the Turkana people in the west and north of Lake Rudolph (now Lake Turkana).

Many cattle, camels and goats had died. Others were driven off by raiders whom a people enfeebled by hunger were too weak to withstand. Looking for solutions, the NCCK surveyed Lake Rudolph to assess fish stocks. They found that it could sustain not only the existing individual offshore fishermen but a fishing industry. A co-operative was accordingly established which involved the development of new skills and capacities to work as a team. It also brought with it small industries such as boat-building, net-mending, fish-curing and handicrafts. The new source of prosperity, based on fish rather than animals, allowed money to be pushed back into old tribal lands.

A success story? My visit in the early 1970s put some question marks.

– There were 'responsible' people who spent their money on goats, cattle and camels which they introduced to the already over-grazed pastures and there were 'irresponsible' people who spent their money on drink and prostitutes. It was the former who did the severest damage to the tribe.
– The new leadership of the fishing community was seen as a threat by the traditional leadership.
– When it became known that higher prices for fish were available in the Congo, fish came to be sold there rather than to the protein-deficient tribespeople, and so the people whom the scheme was designed to benefit lost out.

Often it is only possible to do what one can. Thereafter consequences, foreseen and unforeseen, need to be addressed. This is what we have to learn about participating in the mission of God: there are hills beyond hills. This does not excuse us from tackling the one immediately facing us.

* * *

PRAYER

God the Lord,

Should I live strong and confident because I look to you and trust in you? The truth is that I am often confused and uncertain what to do for the best.

Life is often too disorderly for me to be able to sort it out. How can I hope to take a clear path which expresses your will for my life? Search me and know me, try my heart, see if I am deluding myself and hiding from the truth. My baptism requires me to offer my life to you. I take a step which seems asked of me. Then factors I had not anticipated spoil the outcome. I begin to regret even that first step of faith. If there were a clear choice between a broad and narrow way I might choose the narrow way to life. But where is it?

Lord God, be a lamp to my feet and a light to my path.

God the Lord,

Should Christian aid agencies be strong and confident because they look to you and trust in you, for they are often confused and uncertain what to do for the best? The international scene changes so rapidly that what is planned with compassion and imagination may look ill-judged by the time it is in place. Governments invite and encourage initiatives and then put obstacles in the way if their own interests are threatened. Warring factions interrupt urgent supplies. To feed the starving, life has to be hazarded – often the life of comrades and co-workers. At times agencies to not know where to turn, how to allocate finite resources when faced with a seemingly infinite number of claims. At times, what is done in good faith turns out to be disastrous.

Lord God, how can we serve you in this crazy world?

'Let not the wise man boast of his wisdom, let not the mighty man glory in his might, let not the rich man glory in his riches; but let him who glories glory in this, that he understands and knows me, that I am the Lord who practise steadfast love, justice and righteousness in the earth; for in these things I delight says the Lord.' (Jeremiah 9.23-24)

Lord God, often uncertain what to do for the best, we rest in your sufficiency

Amen.

On another occasion, the National Christian Council of Kenya came to the assistance of people affected by drought in what was largely a Muslim area. The situation was already much mitigated by the faithfulness with which those Muslims who had income set aside 10 per cent for their needy brothers and sisters. The people were reluctant nomads, moving continually in the quest for adequate food supplies but wishing to settle. The NCCK helped them to establish 'training for growth' projects, on an inter-tribal basis, in the hope of producing change towards a stable economy based on agriculture and at the same time of healing tribal wounds.

Technical assistance was offered through missionary agencies. With the resources came missionaries who looked upon Islam as a realm of darkness from which Christ was absent.

Now there was already an African Church in that area. The Christians had a friendly relationship with the Muslims. The attitude of the foreign missionaries threatened to split the human community along religious lines. It also menaced the reconciling potential of the training-for-growth projects. These had been cunningly located on the boundaries of different, often hostile tribes, so that people would learn agricultural skills and learn to respect one another at one and the same time.

Looking at the situation, I questioned a resident technical adviser about the implications: 'Is this a clear case where assistance from others who have different skills is acceptable, on the basis of a common humanity, but a deliberate programme of evangelization is not?' 'No,' he replied, 'they are quite open to evangelization as well. But it has to be evangelization in terms of the impact made by their lives. By that they are prepared to be persuaded. Evangelization by word alone, carrying with it a wholesale and uninstructed condemnation of Islam and of the things Muslims have loved and cherished and respected with all its consequences of divisiveness is something they will not tolerate.'

* * *

PRAYER

'O Lord my God you are very great: you are clothed with glory and majesty, covering yourself with light as with a cloak, stretching out the skies like a tent; who lays the beams of his upper chambers in the waters, who makes the clouds his chariot and walks on the wings of the wind, making spirits his messengers, flames of fire his servants: who established the earth on its foundations.' (Psalm 104.1-5)

Our grasp on you is frail, our understanding incomplete. It is of your mercy that you accept us as we are, who prove to be such inadequate testimonies to your mystery and love.

– Save us from trying to get people to live our way, as if our way were yours.

We are but part of your vast human family, scattered over the face of the earth: our history subsists among many histories, our culture among many cultures, our forms of worship among manifold forms of worship, our language of faith among many languages. Throughout history you have come to people along the path of life which is recognizable to them, so that they appreciate that you are no alien God but their God, their true God.

– Save us from making our apprehension of you final when humankind has such a rich experience to draw on, such a wealth of perceptions of your reality.

We have much growing to do into the stature of the fullness of Christ. We can intrude into people's lives at the wrong time, in the wrong way – concealing Christ when we think that we are commending him. We can be insensitive to what others have to give us.

– Save us from approaching others in ways which turn them from you instead of turning them to you.

You are the God with whom all have to do. Save us from trusting to our little light when Christ is Daylight for humanity.

In his name we ask it
Amen.

CROSSING FRONTIERS

Jesus' choice of downward mobility – his association with outcast and marginalized people – is still a road which his followers may be asked to take.

In 1972, challenged by Jesus' example, ten young people in Lima, Peru, who had trained as teachers and could have been upwardly mobile, decided to live in a deprived community. They put down their roots into the life of the people, accepted their culture, learnt their key words and used these to encourage the development of awareness of their oppressed situation and to encourage choices for freedom.

Four of the teachers took on paid employment. The $72 per month earned by the four had to support the total team and pay for teaching materials and apparatus as well.

They crossed a financial frontier, adopting a simple style of living which allowed the income of a few to do for all. Thus they found an alternative to that of financing by outside agencies.

They crossed an educational frontier immersing themselves among those who had little education or none, honouring their wisdom, enlarging it. They crossed a class frontier, refusing the status available to middle-class professionals, choosing rather to live alongside those who were regarded as belonging to the lowest stratum of society. They crossed a cultural frontier, deliberately refusing to be cultural capitalists; deciding to honour the culture of the lowly rather than the prestige culture for which they could have opted. They crossed a frontier of individualism, for they acted as a team. Four of them came to meet me to make it clear that leadership does not fall to any one of them, but is shared.

* * *

'Jesus said, "Truly I say to you ... everyone who has left houses, or brothers or sisters or father or mother or children, or fields for my name's sake shall receive many times as much and shall inherit eternal life.

But many who are first will be last; and the last, first."'

(Matthew 19.28-30)

SELF-EXAMINATION

Do I look for advancement and promotion? Jesus laid aside his glory and was made of no reputation. What does my baptism ask of me? Never mind assumptions made by others about what counts – am I putting my gifts and education at the service of those to whom God wants to send me?

Am I too much at ease in my class and cultural context? I may be called to move out. Jesus consorted with society's rejects.

As the result of an evangelistic initiative developed by the Mission Department and the local Churches, three families in the Selly Oak community sold their houses and took up residence in the inner city where need was greatest. What is asked of me?

To swim against the tide is costly. The Marcan version of the biblical quotation above adds to Jesus' promise that persecutions might follow. Good people as well as bad made sure that Jesus was crucified. Am I ready to bear my cross?

Leave my family? It is quite likely that Jesus, as the oldest son, helped to rear the family when Joseph died. What confronts Christians is not the demand to break intimate ties as such, but to break 'for my name's sake' any which stand in the way of God's calling. We should ask ourselves 'are there family ties which I should strengthen for his name's sake?' as well as 'are there those which I should break?'; 'is my house so situated that it provides a base for obedient living?' as well as 'should I be moving elsewhere?'; 'am I to claim and use my possessions?' as well as 'should I part with them?' The essential thing is to submit all life and its possibilities to God, and see what is required of us, and then put that before all other demands.

We are not our own. We are bought with a price.

I was brought up in the town of Forres in the North East of Scotland. As a child, I watched the well-dressed folk go to church on a Sunday ignoring the street-corner loungers. As an adolescent, I worked in our family's butcher shop before beginning university and then theological training at New College, Edinburgh. As I approached the end of my training in 1942, I came under strong personal compulsion to try to bridge a gulf and go into industry to work alongside labourers.

The decision to make this venture had been met mainly by mystification or downright incredulity on the part of some. Why on earth had I taken all that training if I were going to throw it away? I had a great chance of an academic future – why on earth should I turn that opportunity down when it was the kind of contribution which the Church needed? I could say my new and strange things in classrooms as profitably as anywhere outside a theological college.

I turned out explanations for journalists and for those who challenged the action, but I really was not clear myself. Looking back, I suppose I was an apostle in that an apostle goes into foreign territory, all eyes and ears to observe what is going on, and stays attentive for the word which will come there from one's authority. All I knew was that I was being drawn in this direction, that, thanks to the collaboration of Dr George MacLeod, Dr David Russell (the proprietor) and the Home Board of the Church of Scotland, an opportunity had been opened out in a mill of 1,200 people – and I just had to go and discover in the actual situation and in God's good time what it was all about.

Some read too much into the action. 'You are really identified with working people,' they enthused. I was quick to disenchant them. 'I have two degrees,' I said. 'These give me escape routes. Most of the folk there have nowhere else to go. They are stuck here for life. So I am not *identified* with them, and never can be with my background and my education. I am *identifying* with them as far as I can, that's all.'

* * *

'Seek first the kingdom of God and his justice and all these things shall be yours as well.' (Matthew 6.33)

REFLECTION

The Kingdom of God is the whole created fabric of life shaped God's way. There will be a struggle throughout history to find what taking God's way means; and yet a greater one to fulfil what that implies.

The words of Isaiah, quoted in Jesus' first sermon and Jesus' Sermon on the Mount (quoted in Luke 4) make it clear that there will have to be a change in human priorities, for which a change of mentalities will also be needed.

Life shaped God's way is placed before us as the first requirement. Everything else can flow from that. But what does that mean, and how is it to be achieved?

If the deprived are to get their share of God's liberal provision, the wants and desires of the well-off will need to be reined in. Cultures are needed which emphasize solidarity, societies which value community, laws which afford justice to all, political measures which ensure that resources are fairly distributed. Yet those who want personal gain find constraints hard to take. Wartime rationing improved the health of people in Britain out of recognition. Yet the bait of 'good red meat' won votes, even though it meant a return to unequal sharing.

The word 'deregulation' quite simply implies loss of control. That is quite acceptable on a scale where things sort themselves out. But where regulation is the only way to ensure the resources of the earth are available for human and other living creatures in reasonable proportion (though there will always be richer and poorer), deregulation is a sign of insensitivity to the will of God for the world. God means us to be in charge of life, for his people's good, and to manage the earth's resources to that end.

Consider the gambling spirit in humanity, its good as well as bad features. Did not Abraham take a gamble in moving out, seeking the Promised Land? In pursuit of a vision, we must often move from where we are.

Pray 'Your Kingdom come, your will be done on earth as in heaven.' Set out to live that prayer, starting from where you are.

A cluster of four villages in Bungsipsee in Chaiyapoon Province in North-East Thailand invited a student team to live with them and work with them for some weeks in the development of their common life. The enterprise attracted students from all the universities of Thailand. It was sponsored by Roman Catholics but Buddhists in the team outnumbered Christians by five to one. Tiny girls who had never handled a mattock or any other agricultural implement in their lives, soon learned the swing which puts the work on the iron head rather than on human arms; and grew adept at working in cement and concrete to make water tanks.

It was an exercise in mutual respect and understanding between people of different faiths. In the morning the Thai flag was raised and people gathered together for a short period of Buddhist prayer and meditation. Each evening, after an evaluation session, the Christians were accustomed to hold an act of worship. After some time Buddhist students said, 'Many of us believe in God too; may we join in?' They were made welcome. Soon Buddhists were reading Old and New Testament lessons, singing hymns, offering prayers as part of a total trusting company.

It was an exercise in human development. The villagers had their lives enlarged while the students learned to respect the wisdom and values of rural people. They went back much more fully developed human beings.

It was an exercise in wholeness. Village sanitation and personal health care, shared manual work, awareness of rural needs, growth in joint action, worship and prayer, Christian/Buddhist understanding, theological reflection – all these strands – were tied into one bundle of life.

* * *

'There is a lad with five barley loaves and two fish; but what are these among so many?' (John 6.9)

'Lord I believe: help my unbelief.' (Mark 9.24)

PRAYER

Father, Son and Holy Spirit, source of ultimate power and ultimate love, you can do exceeding abundantly above all that we ask or think. We praise you that you who are with us are always beyond us, with gifts in store for those who would journey. We bless you that you who are beyond us are always with us, your ears open to our cries. We can look to you with expectation. All that we ask in the name of Jesus Christ will be given: and in the asking and receiving we will get deeper into knowledge of your marvellous will for your whole Creation – even we who are of the earth earthy.

We find it hard to believe that it is when we are weak that we are strong, that it is when we have nothing that we possess all things. Yet a lad put a little food into Christ's hands – and a multitude was fed.

– Forgive us, so preoccupied are we with the inadequacy of what is in our hands that we fail to put it into Christ's.

– Teach us the grace of Mary, available to be filled with Christ.

Our belief in you and what is possible is so limited by what seems proper to ask of you. Teach us again:

'We are coming to a King, large petitions with us bring:

for his grace and power are such none can ever ask too much.'

– Forgive us, so subject to the world's values even when we approach you in whose hands the world rests.

– Teach us the faith of the man with the epileptic son.

Give us heart to venture in your name, Father, Son and Holy Spirit: developing enterprises of hope, investing energy, skill and foresight in preparing them, then putting them in your hands that they might be fruitful to the nourishment and blessing of your whole human family and of your whole Creation.

We ask it in Jesus Christ's name

Amen.

LIFE-GIVING THEOLOGY

As I walked down the street after a political meeting, a young woman caught up with me: 'Can I have a word with you?' she asked. She came to the point straight away: 'Tonight's meeting did it. You never try to hide the belief that motivates you to struggle against injustice. Now, I'm in the same struggles. But I don't have a basis to draw on. More and more I feel the want of that. It grows on me that the source you have is what I am looking for. I'm not a Church person. But I'd like you to talk about the Christian faith with me. Could you come up some evening?' I did so and we talked for some hours. The woman and her husband became clear that the Christian basis for living was what they could affirm.

It was a fight against the Poll Tax which brought Mrs McMenemin and myself together in Stirling. She had been rallying opposition through her secretaryship of the Raploch Tenants' Association. I had been fighting the tax through the courts. I went to her house for an update on her activities. At the end of a long spiel on the effects on poor people, I said to her, 'You've put your finger on the theological basis for resisting the Poll Tax.' 'Have I? What did I say?' 'You said, "God's no' for injustice, God's for folk."' 'Did I? Well, I was right. That is the theological basis for fighting it!'

By the time the Government abandoned attempts to enforce the Poll Tax, my case was before the European Court. At the previous stage, when being judged by three Law Lords in the Court of Session, some frequenters of Gargunnock Inn asked me to tell them about my arguments. I started to do so – the legal argument based on the Act of Union, the theological argument based on requirements of natural justice, the moral argument against partners and neighbours keeping tabs on one another and telling tales. Then I had a better idea: 'I'll tell you what. I'll put a copy of my case against the Poll Tax on the pub counter and you can read it and judge for yourselves.' It was in the local inn that the case, with its theological core, was debated.

There is no end of places appropriate for doing theology – political meetings, resistance struggles, law-courts, pubs!

* * *

REFLECTION

Where shall theology be found and where is the place of understanding?
(cf. Job's question in ch. 28.13)

We are at a new point in history. People at the bottom of the heap in
society are lifting their heads, finding light in the Bible, realizing their
inherent dignity in the eyes of God, developing theological insights
relevant to situations they face, and taking charge of history. Theology
is not being worked out aside from life but in the thick of life. Joel's
prophecy has come true: 'Even on slaves, men and women, will I pour
out my spirit.' (Joel 2.29)

Pray for those who are discovering the life-giving role of theology as the
faith basis for managing life that they may have confidence to play
their part, counting their own language and experience adequate and
appropriate for building up insights into gospel demands and prom-
ises;
– that they may not be overconfident, as if God's mind could be read and
appreciated instantly without a struggle for light;
– that they may be open to the ideas of others who are trying to find a true
path however tentatively, and may honour the contribution of scholars,
and submit their perceptions to one another so as to get nearer the
truth.

Pray for those who feel threatened by this development and tempted to
quench the Spirit;
– that they may learn the exhilaration of the new era Joel prophesied and
be prepared for an exodus from entrenched positions – in a new
community seeking the mind of Christ for our time.

SELF-EXAMINATION

Am I prepared to move from safe ground?
Am I prepared to be open to the ideas of others, that we may search for the
truth more effectively together?

MISSION: PRODUCTIVE OR DESTRUCTIVE?

When I was in Zululand on WCC business, I learnt of one impact of Christian missionary work on the community.

Before missionaries came to that area, the following custom obtained. If a mature young man and young woman were attracted to one another, with the consent of the parents they could summon their friends and discuss the possibility of a sexual encounter. If this was agreed, there were certain rules to be followed. All kinds of sexual play would be allowed except penetration since the young woman would lose her 'brideprice' of cattle if this happened. Usually this would be the only such casual encounter which would take place between the girl and someone she fancied. Most often she would marry someone else.

Into this society came white missionaries. They became aware of this practice and denounced it as a filthy one. If you were a Christian, they said, you must abandon it. They failed entirely to take account of the social basis on which the particular custom rested. In the society everyone was given a grounding in sex education from the earliest years. Imaginatively, instruction for the years when young people matured into adults was made the responsibility of older teenagers. The white missionaries paid no attention to this basis. No alternative sex education was provided. So Christian girls became known as 'easy game'. From that time to this, Christianity and illegitimacy have been linked.

* * *

Dr James Stewart, who became Principal of Lovedale in South Africa in 1870, founded the 'Kaffir Express'. In his second editorial, he wrote, 'Our aim is to scatter ideas in the moral wastes and desert places of heathen ignorance ....'

REFLECTION

A statement on the future of mission originating in the traditional sending areas was made by Bishop F. Pagura to the Missionary Liaison Committee of Costa Rica, where he served until the early 1970s:

– *If you cannot understand what is happening in this continent, in this hour in which it awakens to the dawn of a new liberation, Missionary, go home.*

– *If you are not able to separate the eternal word of the gospel from the cultural moulds in which you brought it to those lands and even taught it with true abnegation, Missionary, go home.*

– *If you cannot identify with the sufferings, anguish and aspirations of these peoples made prematurely old by an unequal struggle that would seem not to have end or hope, Missionary, go home.*

– *If your alliance and fidelity to the nation of your origin is stronger that your loyalty and obedience to Jesus Christ who has come to 'put down the mighty from their thrones and exalt those of low degree' (Luke 1.52), Missionary, go home.*

– *If your dogmatism is such that it does not permit you to revise your theology and ideology in the light of all the biblical testimony and the happenings of these times, Missionary, go home.*

– *If you are not able to love and respect as equals those whom one day you came to evangelize as 'lost', Missionary, go home.*

– *If you cannot rejoice with the entrance of new peoples and churches into a new period of maturity, of independence, of responsibility, even at the price of committing errors such as those you and your countrymen committed also in the past, then it is time to return home.*

But if you are willing to share the risks and pains of this hour of birth which our American peoples are living, even denying yourself;

– *if you begin to rejoice with them because of the joy of feeling that the gospel is not only announcement and affirmation of a remote hope, but of a hope and a liberation that is already transforming history;*

– *if you are willing to put more of your time, of your values, of your life at the service of these people who are awakening,*

then, stay, since there is much to be done, and hands and blood are needed for such an immense enterprise in which Christ is pioneer and protagonist.

The plea, in some cases, for a moratorium – a break in the flow of money, personnel, etc., from richer parts of the world to poorer parts – may not represent hostile action but action for survival and identity. Where the mere presence of Europeans produces impotence, then their best service may be to get right out and to offer those they have sought to serve time and breathing space to develop their own particular form of Christian life. If this brings a time of helpless suffering, of breakdown, that may be the gift that those who have been only too dominating owe to the dominated.

This is what was experienced by the Sabaneto Community in the north of the Dominican Republic. They numbered about ten. In an area where the struggle was to rise to subsistence level, they had to live from hand to mouth, with, at best, irregular employment. Yet they were Christians who were alert to their situation and had become convinced that they should not be victims but rather agents of change in it, in the hope that the whole area might become one of greater justice and opportunity for poor campesinos.

This awakening of new hope had been stimulated and encouraged by the contribution of people from other lands. But the day came when they believed they had to part from their last expatriate worker and, with him, from the skills he brought and the finance which can always be tapped when someone comes from a richer land. Some time later I put this question to them: 'Would you like to have the help of expatriate staff again?'

They thought a while. Outside help had obviously done a great deal for them. Then, one by one, they gave the same answer: 'No. It has been a painful experience, it has been a bit like a death. We have often not known how to carry on. But we now begin to see, at last, that there cannot be resurrection without this death; and we are becoming resurrected as a community who make their own decisions, even though what we can do seems to be so inadequate in face of the needs of this whole area.'

* * *

REFLECTION

God is the great Giver, bestowing life and abundance through Jesus Christ: 'of his fullness we have all received and grace upon grace' (John 1.16). We have nothing that is our own to give. At best we can share in God's giving.

Accordingly when we give or receive, we should not regard some as benefactors and others as beneficiaries for all things come from God and are to be shared with the same unaffected generosity as God has shown to us.

— We should not regard some as superior and others as inferior: for what the 'superior' possess is not owned but loaned for God's purposes; and what the inferior have to give may be more important in quality as in the case of 'the poor of this world, rich in faith.' (James 2.5)

— We should not regard some people as enlightened and others as unenlightened. 'God has chosen the world's foolish things to put to shame the learned; and God has chosen the weak in the world to shame the strong.' (1 Corinthians 1.27)

How can we give without patronizing and receive without deference? Consider as a sign God's giving in Jesus Christ, effected without trumpeting, without making the poor feel inferior, without assuming airs or putting pressure on people to submit: a giving which was unobtrusive, in which outcasts were honoured and given dignity, in which the coming was of one who was 'meek and lowly in heart'.

Then

— Ask God and the victims for forgiveness for the crusading spirit and assumed superiority which has often marked missionary endeavour; and examine your own heart for any arrogance towards other races.

— Ask God and the victims for forgiveness for times when Christians saw themselves as lamps bringing light to heathen darkness, and failed to do justice to what God was already doing in other cultures; and examine your own heart for lack of openness to receive insights from unfamiliar cultures and faiths.

— Ask God and the victims for forgiveness for ways in which development has been understood and aid given in our own time so that the initiatives of indigenous people have been inhibited and their spirit of independence sapped; and examine your own heart for any patronizing elements which may mark your giving, any deference to other than God which might mark your receiving.

VALUING PEOPLE

The Vickers shop stewards on Tyneside were concerned that their skills should be directed towards developing peaceful products. As part of the WCC's 'Participation in Change' programme, I met with them to discuss proposals they had set out in a document entitled 'An Alternative to the Chieftain Tank'. One of their number registered dissent from the others' viewpoints: 'If I was offered overtime to make weapons which I knew would in the future kill my own children I would take it – because it's money in my hand, now.'

Sitting on the floor of a Korean slum, a young man described his efforts to form a trade union outside the work premises after attempts to do this openly and publicly on the shop floor had been frustrated by intimidation and by 'relocating' awkward potential leaders elsewhere. This fresh move had been discovered. He was dismissed from employment in a way which meant that no other firm was likely to take him on. He had been unemployed for six months. No unemployment benefit was available.

'How do you manage to live?' I asked him.

'Fellow-Christians who do not have enough to eat themselves share what they have with me,' he replied.

Outside a vegetable cart passed by. Two small outside leaves of cabbage had fallen off, and the wheels of the cart had pressed them into the mud. A young child retrieved them and was busy scraping the mud off so that they could be used.

* * *

PRAYER

Father, Son and Holy Spirit, you are a society of love and efficiency. You are maker, redeemer, renewer of all created life. What you purpose, you bring to pass. It is in your life that we find life and learn to manage more effectively the world which you have entrusted into our hands.

We pray for managers of industry:

– *so often subject to distant control by head offices;*
– *buffeted by a great variety of pressures in decision-making;*
– *restricted by the ups and downs of their country's performance;*
– *constrained by what is happening in world markets;*
– *faced with decisions which critically affect people's lives;*
– *and irked by interference from those they consider ill-instructed;*
– *also protecting their own interests and tempted to reject power-sharing;*
– *inclined towards short-term results to please shareholders;*

that they may be able to look to communities of faith for understanding;
for sustaining of their integrity under pressure; for upholding when
they are baffled or cast down; for criticism when their policies are
unfair to others,

that the Church may be light and salt and leaven in society.

We pray for trade unionists:

– *when they are thwarted in attempts to form unions;*
– *when they are met with resistance from workforce as well as manage-*
ment;
– *when they are victimized;*
– *when human rights are withdrawn from members;*
– *when members who invest a lifetime of skills are made redundant without*
consultation or explanation;
– *also where they have too much power and bring unfair pressures to*
bear;
– *where they fail the public or other trade unionists or the unemployed;*
– *where money in the hand is the measure of all things;*

that they may be able to look to communities of faith for understanding;
for sustaining of their integrity under pressure; for upholding when
they are baffled or cast down; for criticism when their policies are
unfair to others,

that the Church may be light and salt and leaven in society.

Amen.

DIFFICULT CHOICES: CENTRAL AMERICA

A young man was facing a dilemma. He was a Delegate of the Word (a lay person trained for pastoral work) and a member of the local community council. Here is the position in which he found himself.

A road needs repair. Money must be raised for this in the community itself. The council decides to do this by means of Bingo and a dance. Since he is a Christian who has earned respect from the community, he is entrusted to organize it and to handle the money.

So he finds himself thrust into a position where, because his Christian faith impels him to political commitment, he becomes associated with gambling and with alcohol since drink will be sold at the dance (in an area where alcoholism is a real menace because of machismo drinking by men). Some local people challenge him on the kind of example he is setting.

The alternative would be to withdraw from local politics which, he feels, would contradict his biblical faith.

He is torn two ways.

* * *

'God so loved the world that he sent his only-begotten Son, that whosoever believes in him should not perish but have eternal life.' (John 3.16)

REFLECTION

If God's love is set on the world, that is where his people should be. Since we are found there, there cannot be the clean-handedness that separation from the world would bring. We are faced with compromises, awkward choices, awkward alliances, denied the clear decisions which can be made in the abstract by the uninvolved.

To be separated off for God in the world (the meaning of 'holy') is quite a different matter from being separated off from the world God loves. The Kingdom will not be established and God's will done on earth as in heaven unless life is hazarded on earth.

Jesus got a bad name for morally dubious actions: for showing respect for women in ways which contradicted law and custom; for being found in the company of the unclean and outcasts; and for playing fast and loose with regulations concerning ritual washings and the Sabbath.

PRAYER

Heavenly Father

We give thanks that you did not stay aloof from the ambiguities and perplexities of this mortal life, but took them upon yourself in the life of your Son.

We give thanks that he was found among us, dealing with life as we have to reckon with it.

We rejoice that he too found decisions difficult, gave the wrong impression, was misjudged and ill-thought-of.

We are comforted that it is our humanity, our real humanity, which Jesus Christ bears, transformed in the Godhead.

We bless you that, in the end, it is not what we are in the eyes of human beings but in your eyes which counts.

Forgive us that we look for the clean-handedness which is an alternative to being engaged where it matters; that we shun company at whom our neighbours would raise eyebrows; that, when the chips are down, we steer clear of trouble – even the trouble needed to establish truth and justice; that thus we do not offer our bodies, our whole beings, a living sacrifice acceptable to you which is the true worship you have a right to look for.

Absolve us from our sin, and make us available for whatever work you would entrust to us.

We ask it in Jesus Christ's name and for the sake of the world he loved

Amen.

AN EVANGELICAL NECESSITY

In 1977, when I visited the Philippines, it looked as if I would have to return home without an interview with one person I particularly wanted to meet, Senator Jovite Salonga. He was the man who, after the revolution, was entrusted with the business of tracing the Marcos millions squirrelled away abroad in secret accounts. He was a lawyer, lecturer and lay preacher. He would take up the case of anyone who got rough justice from the Marcos regime, knowing that this made him a political target. He had suffered in jail.

During my visit, he had gone to an island off the coast of the Philippines and was not due to be back until after I was due to leave.

I had just been interviewing Trining Herrera, the leader of the Tondo community, newly released after being tortured, and was in the office of her lawyer at the time. The language being used was Tagalog. I could not help hearing some words which I thought I understood, including the word 'Jovite'. I asked whether by any chance the person at the other end of the line was Senator Salonga. To my delight, I was told that it was.

I asked the lawyer to send Senator Salonga my regards and to say how sorry I was that we were out of reach and that I would not be able to see him. 'But he is back here on the mainland,' I was told. 'He did not intend to be here at all but he has just been telling me that he felt under very strong pressure to return early – that something was wanted of him.' I was able to take the phone and speak to him directly. He was able to meet me for two hours – exactly the two hours which I myself had to spare before leaving for the airport.

One thing that the Senator said will always stay with me. He spoke of 'the evangelical necessity of research into transnational corporations, lest the world get into a powerful grip which is other than God's.'

* * *

REFLECTION

*Christians have no special way of getting knowledge about the facts of
situations they face. They have to do their homework like everyone
else. If they do not, they are at the mercy of all kinds of propaganda
and can be deluded into thinking they carry out God's will when they
only frustrate it.*

*' ... we are no longer to be children, swung back and forth and carried
here and there by every wind of teaching that springs from human
trickery and craftiness in deceitful scheming; but, speaking the truth in
love, we are to grow up in every way into him who is the Head –
Christ.' (Ephesians 4.14-15)*

*An 'evangelical' necessity? The good news of the gospel is for transform-
ing existence as it actually is today. So, what is truly there – not some
imagined substitute – must be identified and reckoned with. Unless we
do tough, detailed work to disclose reality we cannot say how the
gospel should impinge on life as it is lived, on people, on organizations, on nations. For the sake of the gospel, we need accurate research. Effective techniques to achieve this are a gospel requirement.*

*Pray for those whose careful statistical work is directed to the exposure of
features and factors which influence the direction life may take, so that
human beings are given the chance to make instructed decisions.*

*Pray for those who may be under pressure to produce results which suit
government departments, or transnational corporations, or Churches,
or lobbies or other vested interests; especially if they are threatened
with dismissal if they do not comply.*

*Pray for those who struggle to gain theological perceptiveness, assessing
situations and promoting imaginative action, drawing on gospel
insights. Pray for teams which bring different disciplines and skills to
bear on complex problems.*

*Lord God, you have put us in charge of the earth. May we take charge with
open eyes and clear vision.*

We ask it in Christ's name
Amen.

FAITH INVOLVES RISKS (1)

In 1975 people flooded into Nima, Ghana, from the surrounding areas. Services collapsed. The government gave up. The people threw in their hand. Nobody quite knew what to do with all the problems.

Eventually, the government decided to relocate all the inhabitants, and clear the whole area by complete demolition. An evangelical Christian group of students, including my contact James Sarpei, realized that this might simply create another Nima elsewhere. So they moved in. They spent most of their time clearing up the area, removing filthy heaps of refuse. People became curious. They joined in. As they saw that the situation could be improved by their own efforts, they took heart. Students and local people began to talk together, to share problems and hopes.

From this a new spirit developed. Trusted leadership came forward. Apathy gave way to the flowering of community initiative. Given fresh encouragement by the government they appointed two developmental welfare committees to work with the high-powered, top-level government Committee for the Redevelopment of Nima and Malibu.

An indication of the sensitivity of the approach of the Christian team was the good relationships which obtained with Muslims. The latter were fully engaged in the total project, felt they were respected, and knew that when they entered into dialogue about the deep things of life, they would not be manoeuvred on to ground which set them at a disadvantage. A Christian or a Muslim might preside or might start with a prayer at any of their planning meetings, with the acceptance of the total group.

In the Muslim community the young people, with great sensitivity, first consulted the traditional leaders about any plan or proposal. The latter invited young Muslims and Christians to their policy-making sessions. The whole project was a heartening creative development within Islam itself with young people and traditional leaders respecting one another's leadership gifts; and a great step forward in Christian–Muslim relations.

* * *

PRAYER

Lord God you make all things new.

*We long for security. Yet it can be through breakdown that you reach us
and teach us and give us new life – breakdown in personal and working relationships, breakdown in prospects for recognition or promotion, breakdown through strangers invading our privacy and property,
breakdown of societies.*

*– God The Disturber, make us alert to the opportunity to do a new thing
when the old way is withdrawn.*

*We are inhibited by the inadequacy of our resources. Yet a few loaves and
fishes fed thousands. It is not how much we have to give or how little,
but whether we place what we have in Christ's hands.*

*– All-sufficient God, free us from paralysis because of the little we can
offer.*

*We may be uncomfortable working with government and non-governmen-
tal organizations, critical of their poor attempts to remedy situations,
aware of human aspects which they do not seem to take into account.
Yet they in turn have reason to find us often uninstructed, idealistic or
inadequately committed.*

*– God the Lord, help us to work critically and supportively with bodies
appointed to attend to people's wellbeing.*

*We are at a time when people of different faiths seek better to understand
one another and to establish community with one another.*

*– Almighty God, Father and Mother of your whole human family, help us
to journey through life respecting one another, open and teachable
before one another, that we might come to a larger understanding of
you through the shared perceptions of others and together with them
work your will in the world;*

and to you, Father, Son and Holy Spirit be all glory for ever.
Amen.

SELF-EXAMINATION

– my readiness/unreadiness to look to God when things go awry;

– my preparedness to risk action, living by faith not by sight;

– my acceptance of public responsibilities, or shunning of them;

– my openness to people of other faiths and to atheists and agnostics.

FAITH INVOLVES RISKS (2)

In the 1960s the Scottish Churches' House programme planning committee had been keeping an eye on gang warfare in Easterhouse – the housing scheme in Glasgow which lumped blocks of flats together without adding the facilities which are needed to make human life human. Committee members had not been content to wring their hands. Nor did they summon a consultation of the Great and the Good to See What Should be Done. They invited the gangs themselves to meet in Scottish Churches House as their guests.

They knew the risk they were taking – walls covered with aerosol slogans and other graffiti, fights, broken windows, broken furniture, blood spilled. Since ground-floor bedrooms at Scottish Churches House had windows giving direct access to the street, disturbance could spill out into the community and the committee themselves would have to take the rap.

Three of the four gangs accepted, and were well represented. Members met and talked through their concerns but in a discontinuous way which was very strange to those of us accustomed to orderly procedures. They could not sit still for any length of time. There was a constant stream of people leaving the discussion room and a return stream of those rejoining the conversation. Yet the members managed to take stock of their situation, listen to one another's viewpoints as never before, and find some common ground.

On leaving, one young man got hold of me. 'You've fairly spoiled things, sir,' he said. 'How?' I asked. 'Ach, you can't put a knife in a boy once you lived under the same roof wi' him.'

It was some time before the reality of his remark dawned on me. What the young man had been saying amounted to this. 'Look, in the wasteland of Easterhouse the only colour we get in life comes from violence. To belong to a gang and fight other gangs gives us a sense that we matter. You have taken that away. You have not done anything to change Easterhouse.'

* * *

PRAYER

Let us pray

– *for those who live in situations of violence (ourselves included if it applies); who fear approaching footsteps, knowing that what awaits is bruising and battering; who are in the power of bosses or gang leaders; who are at the mercy of pimps or drug dealers;*

– *for those who fear for their children, lest hostility directed to themselves as parents might be diverted to little ones;*

– *for those for whom the violence of gang life provides the only colour in drab surroundings, their existence otherwise featureless; who do not worry about wounding others and being wounded because life-and-death clashes at least have life in them;*

– *for those whose trade is violence; for soldiers often frightened, often sick at what they are asked to do or pulling a curtain down on it so that they can attempt to hide from themselves what it does to them; or revelling in the power given them in boot and bullet – who do our violence for us and may be made scapegoats for guilt which should be laid at our door; for arms dealers; for governments which starve and kill due to inequitable terms of trade imposed on weak nations;*

– *for those whose violence is directed not to promote but to contain violence through offering resistance to unjust laws and oppressive governments; for UN peace-making and peace-keeping initiatives;*

– *for soldiers who set themselves limits; for whistleblowers; for dissidents and heretics; for all who would give life colour;*

– *for those who restrain – neighbours who respond to cries of distress; Women's Aid refuge centres; voluntary organizations which give support to the vulnerable; police; and hospital staff.*

Amen.

VALUES AND THE CHURCH

One can come across an unbelievable integrity in people.

A group of about twenty-five people in Lima, Peru, several of them bakers, wanted to form a co-operative to provide bread at a reasonable price, and then go on to develop similar co-operatives elsewhere. The possibility of getting capital from abroad to provide machinery was examined. Such finance was viewed by members of the community as representing nothing more than a return to their land of some of the riches which, throughout history, had been taken from them.

But they distrusted agencies of all kinds. When it was suggested to them that the World Council of Churches might provide the finance to get them started they reacted negatively. 'We have been manipulated for long enough and in all kinds of ways,' they said. 'No organization, Christian or otherwise, ever gives money without wanting its own ends served. Everything has strings attached.' As their resources ran right out they kept alive a small flame of hope and a great vision with no idea how these might be realized, but maintaining an absolute refusal to sell their soul.

As long as some of them were employed, they shared among the whole community the earnings of the few. But gradually more and more became workless. One of my contact co-ordinators in Peru was visited by two members of the co-op. – an ex-priest and a social worker. They had nothing more to live on. He had had a birthday the previous day and offered them two pieces of cake, knowing that they probably had had practically nothing to eat that day. They refused it. He pressed them, stressing the fact that they would thus be joining him in his birthday celebration. The ex-priest replied, 'What would our stomachs feel like if we raised their expectations by giving them delicious food like that, and then made them face the want of tomorrow?' So they refused the food. They also refused a loan of money. 'We must learn to live at the level of our impoverishment,' they said.

* * *

PRAYER

Father, Son and Holy Spirit

We marvel at you. You search us all, lay bare what is really in us, judge us, heal us, touch us to new life. Nothing is hidden from you; nothing lies outside your love and your power to forgive and restore. With you lies our undoing, with you lies our mending.

Father and mother to us all

We confess a Church too taken up with its own concerns when, before all else, its concern should be that your will be done on earth as in heaven; a Church unprepared for the cost of fighting for a just, fair, equal, peaceful world;

– and we confess that we are part of that Church and in different ways let you and fellow human beings down.

Christ the Son, our brother

We confess a Church concerned for its own good name when, for the world's salvation, you made yourself of no reputation; a Church called to be your body on earth but unprepared to offer what is genuine worship – being a living sacrifice for the world's healing and salvation (Romans 12.1);

– and we confess that we are part of that Church and fail to spend our lives gladly as you spent your life for us.

Holy Spirit of God

We confess a Church which likes its securities and plans a safeguarded future for itself;

– and we confess that we are part of that Church and are unwilling to go out, as Abraham and his household did, not knowing where they would end up, believing only that you would be with them.

The Church is still your Church. We are still your people. You are rich in mercy. Undo us by your judgement. Mend us by your mercy. That, as your forgiven people, we may yet live to your glory and praise, and that the human family may discern your true face even in us.

We ask it in Jesus Christ's name
Amen.

THE POOR, RICH IN FAITH

INTERVIEW WITH A PRIEST WORKING WITH
AN INDIAN BASIC CHRISTIAN COMMUNITY, GUATEMALA, 1980

'The particular group that I'm talking about meets once a week for Bible reflection. They take some passage from the Bible, read it, meditate on it, discuss it at length, and then try to see how that particular passage can be applied to their everyday life. As a result of their shared faith in the risen Lord, they seek to pinpoint some action that all the members of the community can take. It might be some social action such as going out and helping the poor in some way; or it might be something completely different. That would depend on the community and on the outcome of the reflection that they had had.

'There is a priest who attends the community with some frequency. Perhaps once every six weeks they will get together and, within the framework of their ordinary meeting, they will also have a Mass.'

'I know of another Indian community of very, very poor people. They live in cardboard shacks under a bridge on the outskirts of Guatemala city. A small group of eight people, they get together, once again with the Bible as a basis. They read the Bible and they try to apply what they read to their lives. It's a very small community. It's one that should be growing, and hopefully it will grow. Their group discussions usually lead them to take some kind of action to help all the folk who live under the bridge – there are about fifty or sixty families living in that area in cardboard huts. One of their recent actions was to go to the Town Hall in Guatemala city and demand clean water for all these people. They live there without any water, except when it rains. They would see that initiative as an action flowing from their Christian commitment, from Jesus' commitment to the poor. They say that if they aren't working for these others, what's the point of working at all.'

* * *

PRAYER

Lord God, you humble me before the poor.
The more I have the more I want to cling to.

Jesus Christ did not grasp at divine equality but laid aside his glory,
stripping himself of privilege and security to live life with the conditions
*   we live under;*
he was a vulnerable child, unprotected from Herod's wrath, a refugee;
he was found alongside the lowest, the least, the lost,
he gave all, even life itself.
Yet I hesitate to part with some of my abundance.

Lord God, you humble me before the poor
who when they have a little to eat, share it,
who will fight to secure others' good,
who, having nothing, yet seem to possess all things.

What must I do to be saved?
If we all become poor, there would not even be a portion for each.
I cringe away from the sacrifice Jesus asked of the rich young man. But I
*   also believe I am not called to part with my possessions as he was.*
Or am I? Search my heart, you who know my innermost thoughts.

Teach me so to handle the possessions you have entrusted to me that
*   whatsoever is asked of me, they will be treated as yours, not as my*
*   own;*
– teach me grace to give whatever you require of me, and grace to refuse
*   whatever mistaken pressures guilt would exact from me;*
– teach me to fight unjust systems which rob people of their share of
*   God's provision;*
– teach me to be alert to rationalizations and evasions in my own life and
*   in Church and in public life;*
– teach me not to want to keep the poor in poverty as a sign and re-
*   minder to others, as if merely by being poor they formed a saving*
*   remnant. May I respond to Mary's vision – of the poor lifted high.*

All this I ask in Jesus Christ's name and for his sake
Amen.

THE POOR HONOURED

In Nochinagar, Madras, the palm-leaf huts of the poor people were frequently inundated with sea water or destroyed by fire. The Slum Clearance Board was faced with a choice of rehousing people on higher ground right where they were, next to a beautiful beach, or developing the area for tourism. The Board decided that the poor people were entitled to their location by the beach and set about making their accommodation secure.

The people already had a good structure of community government – office-bearers were elected by popular vote every three years. This aided the relocation process. All the dwellers were given identification cards to prevent outsiders from slipping in and benefiting.

The sensitive ways in which an official body (the Slum Clearance Board) could deal with poor people was illustrated in the following features of its action.

– The slum dwellers cleared away their own huts, being paid a small sum for doing so. The psychological effect was great – demolition was not by outside action but by their own hands, by their own choice.

– They were given permission to build other huts around the building site and each got a gift of 150 palm leaves for doing so. This meant firstly that they re-formed their community without delay, and secondly that they acted as overseers of the work and made sure that the builders kept on the job.

– Allocation was to be by ballot. Some protested that they wanted relatives or neighbours to be located near them. The Board agreed to this adjustment where it was desired and proved possible.

––They were allowed to keep their animals. This was both welcomed and was a cause of quarrels, e.g. hens dirtying neighbours' floors.

One snag was that the women used to go out early and, below the tide line, squat, defecate and exchange news. They were now confronted with a toilet seat and four bare walls! This broke community. It meant a loss of communication concerning who needed help. On a second visit, I found the matter solved. Streets had been made spacious. People had begun to meet at street corners and exchange news. They could look after one another as they had done previously.

* * *

PRAYER

Lord God Almighty

You efficiently control the onward march of the life of this universe and do so with grace; you effectively dealt with our sin in the incarnation of Jesus Christ and made that grace visible in the way he went about life; through the grace of the Holy Spirit you will, without fail, bring us to our promised destiny. Teach us ways of managing life on earth which are both efficient and full of grace such as yours.

We ask it in Jesus Christ's name

Amen.

Pray for planners that they may not be too obsessed with their own schemes but sensitive to the views of those who will have to live with the results of their work;

– pray for bureaucrats, that they may so implement policies that those who are planned for may be accorded dignity and voice;

– pray for government agencies which supply finance, that they may learn to exercise good oversight which is unobtrusive and does not humiliate those who benefit from it;

– pray for field-workers and social workers and all who manage change so that it may fall gently on the vulnerable;

– pray for those who toil and build in order that others might have shelter from storm and fire;

– pray for families and communities facing change, holding together and caring for one another as new demands are made on them and new options open out.

Give thanks for planners, bureaucrats, field-workers and social workers, government agencies, construction engineers, craftsmen and basic labourers whose work carries the world forward – especially where they are given little credit or thanks; who need to hear that their work is blessed in measure as it honours your name and blesses your human family.

Amen.

THE COST OF SOLIDARITY

The story is set in the autumn of 1982 in Kabankalan in the Philippines. Margaret and I had spent most of the evening before his arrest with Fr Brian Gore, an Australian priest. The next day he went to Bacolod. There the military tried to seize him but the bishop of the area – Bishop Fortich – showed great courage and insisted that *he* would deliver his priest to the military centre in Kabankalan with dignity. Bishop and priest returned to Kabankalan with lay workers who were also to be arrested. We joined hundreds of people, who, singing hymns defiantly, walked with them to where soldiers in military carriers, guns at the ready, ringed the centre where the hand-over took place.

The charge related to bullets and a grenade allegedly found in Brian Gore's room. 'It must have been a rubber grenade,' said Bishop Fortich. 'The first report said that it was found in a drawer of a filing cabinet, the next that it was on top. It must have bounced!' The trial dragged on. Eventually the charges were shown to be fabrications.

We knew the real reason for the arrests. In conversation the previous evening Brian Gore had told us of the basic Christian communities which had developed in the mountains and the nearby plain, and of how a poor malnourished people had learned to form co-operatives to gain more adequate return for their labour. The Bible was now in their hands and was a source of life. They met in it a God who set his face against injustices such as they experienced. Nothing is more unwelcome to those wielding power unjustly than awakened, thinking human beings.

Little as they had to sustain them daily, Fr Gore's people went on a twenty-four hour hunger strike. They assembled at 2a.m. in the mountains and walked twelve miles the day after the arrest, to participate in a Mass in the town square. They entered Kabankalan in daylight, a ragged and determined army carrying banners.

The leading banner announced their cause: 'Hunger Protest – Hunger for Justice'.

* * *

'Blessed are you when they slander and persecute you and falsely accuse you of every wrong because of me. Rejoice and be glad for your reward in heaven is great, for so persecuted they the prophets which were before you ....

'You are the light of the world. A city set on a hill cannot be hidden. Nor do folk light a lamp and put it under a cover but on a lamp-stand; and it gives light to all who are in the house.

'Let your light so shine before others that they may see your good works and glorify your father who is in heaven.'
(Matthew 5.11-12, 14-16)

REFLECTION

– *We are called to shine. Wherever we are, those around us should be stirred into seeing things as they really are instead of living in darkness and ignorance. Do we do our homework on situations to expose what is really there, and bring the light of faith to bear on that?*

– *Through us, people should be helped to find their way – not our way but their way – to take decisions about how they go about life. Do we free people we contact to take their way?*

– *Thanks for light should not be directed to us. God should be given the glory.*

– *Slander, false accusation, persecution may be our lot. Do we reckon with these as possible consequences? Do we sometimes ascribe slander, false accusation, persecution to righteous action, when they stem from wrong headedness, bad-timing or ill-judged action?*

PRAYER

Worthy is the Lamb who was slain to receive power and riches and wisdom and might and honour and glory and blessing.

Lord Christ, you hazarded your life to bring us life. We bless you for the Church where signs of the Kingdom appear – in basic Christian communities, in co-operatives, in the weak and powerless fasting and carrying banners to outface the powerful. This is your doing and it is wonderful in our eyes. 'To him who sits upon the throne and to the Lamb be blessing and honour and glory and dominion for ever and ever.' (Revelation 5.12)

Amen.

WHO STANDS WITH US?

Hong Kong, 1973. I was in an area of barrows and stalls in side-streets which left very little space for traffic. Originally those who pitched the stalls had legitimate access to a piece of land which had now been made into a children's playground. A substantial number of that extruded community had an official licence for street trading, but unemployment was so bad that a large number of unlicensed hawkers accumulated around. All the traders had to bribe the police to be free of molestation, and those who had no permits had to pay heavier bribes.

The street traders had been feeling thoroughly depressed and helpless until they saw the way in which the chairman of the Hong Kong Christian Industrial Committee had been speaking out on behalf of the poor. The traders asked the Committee if they would come to their aid directly. My contact, Raymond Fung, answered their plea. What they wanted was space where they could organize a proper market again. They believed the government, were it not continually diverted by the high prices that could be obtained for land for development, could provide a site for them where an old building stood.

An act of 'mission' had proved to be necessary. Someone from outside the situation had to come into it with resources – not to take the struggle over from them, but to strengthen and advise.

When I asked them why, when they believed in a Chinese god who they treated as too remote to bother them, they had such a high regard for the Christian Industrial Mission, they answered, 'When the police harass us, who stands between us and the police? When we are taken to court, who stands beside us?'

* * *

'High above all nations is the Lord, and his glory is exalted above the heavens. Who is like the Lord our God, who is enthroned on high, who looks down upon the heavens and the earth? He raises up the poor from the dust and lifts the needy out of the ash heap to have them sit by the side of princes, with the noblest of his people.' (Psalm 113.4-7)

'The Spirit of the Lord is upon me, for he has anointed me to preach the gospel to the poor; he has sent me to announce release to the captives and restoration of sight to the blind, to set free the downtrodden and to proclaim the year of the Lord's favour.' (Luke 4.18-19)

PRAYER

The kingdom, the power and the glory are yours, O God most high. No kingdoms of the earth can usurp your reign over your Creation. Nations which trust in their own strength crumble to dust. Your kingdom alone is an everlasting kingdom. Your dominion alone endures through all generations. All earthly powers must bow before you. For what can human beings, who are like grass which flourishes and is gone, create to endure that is not done in your strength? You alone do wonderful things who are God the Lord most high. We bow in awe before your majesty.

Yet you who are so high stoop low to hear and bless us. Especially you cherish the poor – harassed by authorities, scarcely surviving, defeated and forlorn, those whom Jesus called your beloved 'little ones'. He was found among them blessing, healing, liberating. We bow in awe before his persistent love, which revealed your heart.

Forgive us that we rest so little in the final grace which shaped the universe.

Forgive us that we trust so little your fatherly/motherly concern for us.

Forgive your Church that it is so rarely found alongside the poor, and bless it when it is:

that there may be a sign before the people of this earth

– of a kingdom of grace and peace;

– of a power which bows low in love;

– of a glory which does not dazzle but delights

that all nations may turn to you to find life

that the earth might be filled with the knowledge of you

as the waters cover the sea

Amen.

EMPOWERING THE POWERLESS

In 1973 I spent some time with the PECCO team – the ecumenical team of Christians who worked and lived among the Tondo community of shanty dwellers on the foreshore of Manila in the Philippines. Under Marcos, basic Christian communities were hated and harassed, for it was here that poor people discovered they were worth much in the eyes of God, and heard the calling to share in shaping the world God's way. They no longer sat tamely under injustices.

Sister Victricia of the Sisters of the Holy Spirit told me about the team's aim to help the people to value and bring into play their own latent resources, empowering them to fight for basic rights such as buying the land where their shacks were erected.

'In spite of what you say,' I observed, 'you are bound to be manipulating them. The members of the PECCO team have education, know-how, the protection of Christian orders and institutions which the shanty-dwellers don't have. Whatever your good intentions you must be holding the strings.'

She drew herself up to her full height, which brought her about level with my shoulders, looked me in the eye, and said firmly, 'You're wrong!' She went on to illustrate: 'We open their eyes to their situation of oppression till they can denounce it in their own words and their own way. Then we shut up. Again, we don't ask why clean water should not be provided for all. We ask them, rather, why a water pipe which stops at such a point should not be extended to another five dwellings. They get together and make out a case. A date is fixed. They find themselves in a room with a rug on the floor and a man behind a desk! Nervously they blurt out some points. They become aware that they have a case. They begin to state it cogently. It dawns on them that the official figure behind the desk might be a bit afraid of them! They win their point.

'The great thing is to encourage them to tackle something which they can argue for and deal with successfully. That gives them confidence. Then you step out of their way and let them get on with it.'

* * *

REFLECTION

God's action in human history is marked by sensitive interference. God has not left us to our own devices, to work ill on one another and to destroy the world, but has taken a hand in human affairs. Yet not so as to dominate and compel. God remains invisible, waits to be turned to – as when the Hebrew people cried out because of the harshness of their bondage in Egypt, and were heard. God hears cries not just prayers!

Yet, in time, when the same people were settled, a priestly system was developed under which women, the poor, the handicapped were harshly dealt with.

God took a different way, sending Jesus that a new relationship with human beings might be established. He came that all might have life and have it more abundantly. He did not ask people to live by new regulations but by the new commandment to love one another. The Holy Spirit enabled people to live his way. They were freed into new life by the Spirit's indwelling.

SELF-EXAMINATION

Think of systems in which you are involved – industrial, political, social, religious – and of the need of people to be liberated into full, responsible life.

Are people made remote from one another or helped to play a full and thoughtful part in shaping life together?

Is the risk God took of giving all human beings responsibility expressed in the way that that particular system allocates responsibility?

Think of the delicate skill required to interfere to release others rather than to make them subject; of the need to give support and to withdraw at the right time that they might stand on their own feet with new confidence in God and in themselves.

What personal action needs to be taken to strengthen or challenge the practice of some organization in which you are involved? Offer to God your willingness to seek change in a way which respects those affected.

ABORIGINAL INITIATIVE (1)

In 1971, TB, leprosy and other diseases flourished among Australian aborigines on a scale which would be considered a scandal if it happened among white people. The infant mortality rate was one of the worst in the world; educational provision was very inadequate; white state officers could overrule aboriginal councils; and magistrates could place an 'assisted' category on an Aborigine and then control his or her movements.

Towards the end of that year the first aboriginal march of protest took place in Brisbane. The object was a symbolic take-over of the office of the official in charge of Aboriginal Affairs – to highlight his unwillingness to meet face to face with their representatives, to draw attention to the fact that he and others could overrule the most solemn and unanimous decisions of their Council, and to force the public to think of the very poor treatment the original Australians received compared with whites. An estimated two hundred marched through the streets, breaking windows and declaring to everyone that they had had enough. The confrontation with the forces of law and order came about as they drew near their goal, and, in the scuffles which broke out, nine were arrested.

To prepare for this manifestation of their growing anger, they met in church for a service of worship, and for a last-minute check-up on strategy and tactics.

'Why should you go to church first of all?' I asked.

My question was met with surprise: 'What is there to do in a situation like ours,' an Aborigine replied, 'except commit your cause to God and then go out and get your heads broken by the police?'

* * *

PRAYER

Pray for indigenous people across the world:

– treated as if they were not made in the image of God, who have an inalienable right to dignity and voice and place;

– disregarded in technically advanced world economies – whose exponents need to be teachable before their sensitive relationship to the land and to one another;

– assimilated to cultures which regard themselves as superior, in which their values and customs are cheapened or set aside;

– dislocated from the life around them, taking refuge in drink or drugs to ease their desperation;

beloved by you as if there were no one else in the world.

Forgive us for the way in which we devalue people who have very different lifestyles from our own

and destroy a significant part of the richness and colourfulness of the creation which you have given for our delight and our instruction.

Teach us to be children of the Father from whom the whole family in heaven and earth derives its name and nature.

We ask it in Jesus Christ's name

Amen.

Pray for police here and elsewhere:

– both turned to and distrusted;

– asked to carry out orders without being given the chance to debate their rights and wrongs;

– seeking to balance caring and law-enforcing tasks;

– given powers which can corrupt;

– through misplaced loyalty, covering up one another's misdeeds;

beloved by you as if there were no one else in the world.

Forgive us for the way in which we feel free to turn to the police and to disown them, at one and the same time;

– failing to uphold them when they act rightly;

– failing to insist that they be disciplined when they demean their profession;

– failing to stand up for those they victimize.

We ask it in Jesus Christ's name

Amen.

RECLAIMING ONE'S INHERITANCE

The Gurindjis, an aboriginal tribe in Australia, had their tribal lands taken away and leased by the government to a British-based company which developed a big cattle station. The aboriginals became stock-men and cattle hands. Their pay was subsistence provision – little more than flour, sugar and tea. Their own life was lived on terms which others imposed. No voice of Christian protest was raised. In 1966 they quietly walked off the land *en masse*.

They could not be lured back by the offer of better wages. They had lost things much more precious than money. Their need was nothing less than to regain identity with themselves and with the sacred land.

What they sought was what still lived in their bones: the knitting up of their own world with that of their ancestors; the restoration of the old community form of organization which allowed them to live with dignity as brothers and sisters, sharing possessions; the burial of the boss/worker division between human beings. Their Moses was Vincent Lingiari. Their wilderness was a dry river bed. Manna was food brought by students and voluntary organizations to sustain their life when it looked as if they must starve. Their Promised Land was Wadi Creek where, again with quiet assurance, moving out in due time from the river bed, they fenced in part of their own land and began there to build their houses, rear their cattle and develop their own style of communal life. They made no secret of their intention – to take back their land a bit at a time. The quiet authority of their act, as they went about it without a weapon in their hands, in the end overcame opposition. The Government took back the leased land from the British Company and secured it for them.

But white-claimed Australian land never passes easily to the meek. It has to be reclaimed by the meek using the power of their power-lessness.

When people are deprived of their own land, denied their traditional life-in-community, broken off from the precious living relationship with the dead, given no alternative but to work for a pittance – and no Christian voice is raised, how can Christianity be understood as other than an accomplice in enslaving transactions?

* * *

'He causes grass to grow up for the cattle

fruits and vegetables for human cultivation

that he may bring forth food from the earth.' (Psalm 104.14)

'The creation was subjected to futility not of its own will

but because of him who subjected it in hope ...

that the creation also itself will be set free.' (Romans 8.20-21)

PRAYER

Mysterious, wonderful, creative God, who in Jesus Christ was shown to be our friend, we marvel at the variety of the world's life, its interdependence, the intricacy of its sustaining. In wisdom you have made it all. In love you have placed in our hands the guardianship and promotion of its varied and colourful existence.

Yet you have not entrusted it to us to do whatever we want with it. You have given it a life of its own. That life waits for its fulfilment on the hope that one day we will come to our senses, recognize that we are stewards not owners of the earth and its resources, and relate so sensitively to it that it will share in the destiny which you have prepared for all that you have made.

You have raised up peoples whom we insensitively label 'primitive' who are a sign of true relationships between natural, animal and human life. Often they have been despised and set aside as Christ was. Yet they have continued, in his spirit, to give testimony to a fullness of life which is hidden from the arrogant and powerful. They point a way of promise, quietly, insistently. We bless you for them

Forgive us whenever we fail to appreciate the earth as your living Creation and have treated it as a mere source of raw materials to be exploited, unmindful of the fact that you have provided abundantly for our real need, and that when we damage it we damage ourselves.

Forgive us whenever we are as unwilling to learn from societies which respect the land and relate to it as to something which has its own valid life; that we have looked on those as backward who point the way forward for us.

Convert us to your will and ways, we pray

Amen.

A GOOD REVOLUTION

'This is too good a revolution for it to be allowed to succeed.' That was my verdict on the Nicaraguan experience after attending the celebrations on the first anniversary of the overthrow of the dictator Somoza.

A good revolution! To stay as I did in the Barrio Ciudad Sandino, Managua was to get clear confirmation that the revolution was the fruit of a people's uprising. The gathering in the great square was to start in the early morning. From 2.30a.m. lorries were already transporting people of the barrio into the centre. Their shouts of joy at liberation confirmed their ownership of the revolution. When the guerillas had come down from the hills, members of basic Christian communities in Ciudad Sandino had rallied to join them and attacked the dictator's armoured cars (supplied by Britain) with sticks and stones, for want of more formidable weapons. From the platform Fidel Castro urged the people to develop their own revolution their own way – but also to learn from mistakes made by the Cuban revolution.

It was a unique experience to see the army march past with their modest, basic equipment. They were greeted with waves of love. This was no triumphalist military parade. This was the people themselves receiving a response of grateful thanks from the people themselves.

Fr Xabier Gorostiaga, who had been a Wiliam Paton Fellow at Selly Oak Colleges was now responsible for economic policies in the new Nicaragua. He held a press conference. There he said that necessities would be put before luxuries; the private sector would be given freedom to operate within the field of priorities decided by the government; land would be shared out to the landless.

This was too big a threat to world powers. They developed counter-measures. Give the revolution a bad name. Use blockades to interfere with supplies. Develop a Contra army to destabilize the country and force recourse to scarce foreign currency for weapons. Finally, interfere blatantly in the electoral process.

People at last voted out the Sandinistas.

Look how the Hebrews reacted in the wilderness. After the rigours of the desert, slavery in Egypt appeared attractive.

* * *

PRAYER

God the Lord

*Why do you allow great promise, produced at the cost of sweat and blood
and so much sacrifice, to be destroyed – you who are claimed to be in
charge?*

*Why do you trust people like us, who have let you down so often, to do
right?*

Why will you not answer our questions and make some sense of it all?

Maybe we need to start with a different perspective on life, as Job did.

*We stand in awe before your majesty and love, before the incredible
project of creating the universe and redeeming it; remembering that in
face of your power the nations are like a drop in a bucket and if you
but raised a finger against them they would fall apart; that it is of
your mercy that we are not all consumed.*

Yours is the kingdom and power and glory, yours alone.

*Yet you have made a covenant with us, establishing partnership in your
mission of love. To override us in that partnership would be to reject
us. How you must be cut to the quick with our false talk, our lust for
power, our despising and oppression of your little ones, our crushing of
lifestyles which threaten our own. The cross must have been at the
heart of your life from the moment you chose to make a covenant with
us. We confess that we have not taken into our own hearts the grief of
our God, the cost of solidarity with us, your long patience.*

*Enable us to lighten your heart by fighting to establish justice on earth,
that your wounds may be healed by our answering love and obedience.*

We ask it in the name of the Crucified
Amen.

LIFE SHARED

'It is in the very nature of basic Christian communities that every community has its own special character. They are not clones. Of the seven hundred groups that are in Waiwaitenango, Guatemala, there are seven hundred different kinds. So it would be very difficult to say that there is a model or type which you could label as standard. The exception, however, is that in the Altiplano area of Guatemala, they are all based on Indian culture and on the Indian concept of society. They are Indian communities which get together in an Indian manner, pray in an Indian way, celebrate faith in an Indian way; and members help one another, develop mutual support, in an Indian way. Each basic Christian community in Guatemala would be quite distinctive in the way it expresses its life, while still showing marks of kinship with those in other parts of Guatemala and the wider world.

'For example, in a village, when it is time to thatch a roof, all the members of the community get together to help with that roof. It becomes a form of celebration; and through working together they are creating community. The raw material of community can be found when people get together to perform a task such as sowing seed or thatching a roof; as in the United States during the time of the early colonies when they had quilting bees. The women of the community would get together to make a quilt. That quilt became a symbol of the community. So the thatched roof on a house is a symbol of community or the crop that's about to be harvested is a symbol of community. When you take into consideration that corn is the staple food for many people, the crop that they sow and harvest is a symbol of all that their community is and all that they hope it will be. It is a very powerful symbol.

'In that way, in an Indian way, the Indians celebrate community and form basic Christian communities in a way very different from what people in the city would do. Urban people have a different type of culture. Kinship of these two types with one another comes from their being products of one Spirit.'

* * *

PRAYER

Father, Son and Holy Spirit

You are basic community. Your relationship of love and mutual self-giving is the foundation of all true human community. That gives hope.

We give you praise that you are not content with your own society but call us to share in it. We bless and thank you for the love which takes such a risk. May we live in you, that the communities we form may not be based on superficial attraction, but rest on your own mutual delight in self-giving.

Teach us to accept one another as Jesus Christ has accepted us – in our differences, in our awkwardnesses, in our peculiarities – that a building of God may be firmly made out of different-shaped stones. Enable us to accept one another just as we are, not trimmed into smooth conformities.

Lead us to awareness of our uniqueness, of the identity you give us and the destiny you prepare for us. May we all take shape according to what you have in mind for us, and lend this as a strength to others.

Help us, in an age of individualism, to discard opportunities for getting on for ourselves at the expense of others.

Enable us, in families, to honour each person's particularity and need for space – for you are three; and to show mutual concern and seek to live together in unity of spirit – for you are one.

Bring nations into new community with one another, strengthening the agencies which provide means for international peacemaking.

Since the Church was brought into being to be a sign, instrument and foretaste of the Kingdom of justice, truth and peace which is penetrating the whole fabric of human society,

grant that it may look to you for life

and be to others a community of love and self-giving.

And to you, Father, Son and Holy Spirit, be glory in the Church and in Christ Jesus throughout all ages

Amen.

CHILDREN AND ADULTS TOGETHER (1)

INTERVIEW WITH MARTA MAZARRASA, MADRID, 1980

Q. Children in your congregation, which is also a basic Christian community, are not really thought of as pre-adults who will one day be able to take their full part in Church life. They have a very full part as it is.

A. They usually participate in the sermon on Sundays. The priest, using the roving microphone, introduces the theme which we are to talk about; then they ask questions and also give their own ideas about the theme. The adults also give their reflections. This creates a climate of fraternal warmth where the child feels very happy, finding that he or she has a place in the worshipping community.

Q. Does this mean that the priest acts much more as a kind of co-ordinator of insights, during the sermon?

A. Exactly. The priest, the week before, meets with three families and they discuss with the children what they should concentrate on. Then the theme is presented on Sunday and the rest of the community participates. The priest takes up a position in the middle of the congregation and makes the microphone available.

Q. Both praying and preaching in public worship are things for children?

A. Yes. During the Mass the children can offer petitions and any other prayers that may occur to them.

Q. What happened when eight-year olds were received into full membership of your Church? (I was impressed.)

A. It was even more participative and quite symbolic. They came into church with placards they had made saying they wanted to be members of the community, they wanted to know more about Jesus, and be more fraternal. I find that the children share their own thinking on the faith with one another in the preparation process. That is very significant for them. In the preparation the priest and the children work together.

* * *

'It was you, O God, who brought me forth from my mother's womb; you led me to trust you when I was on my mother's breasts: upon you I was cast from birth, you have been my God from my mother's womb.' (Psalm 22.9-10)

PRAYER

Father, Son and Holy Spirit, you are a family of love. From that love, all Creation was born. By that love all Creation is nourished and sustained. In that love Creation makes growth and matures. Through that love we can grow into the fullness of the stature of Jesus Christ and Creation can be re-created.

We bless you for children entrusted to us, whether born to us or to others who are in community with us: each one special, distinctive in the whole of human history – their birth an incredible unmatched event in the whole process of ongoing Creation. What a wonder it is that you should trust to us the care of their frail lives.

We pray for those who cannot cope; who are overwhelmed by the ceaseless demands of children; who are wearied night and day by their cries; who find no space for their own lives; who are tempted to turn to violence. Give them resilience. Give us imagination to stand by them.

We bless you that, from early years, children can turn to you, recognizing in you the source of love they find in parents and friends; that they can learn to trust you; that, sharing with one another what they have found in you, they can grow in faith; that they can instruct adults and preach and pray with them in the worship and life of the Church.

We bless you that you watch over young people growing up, who are finding life opening out before them, finding strengths and temptations which are new to them, finding relationships which delight and worry them.

We pray for parents and adolescents who find it difficult to relate to one another, for young people who are loners by choice or by circumstances, for those under severe pressures of examinations or sex or drugs.

Help us to found our lives on your life, Father, Son and Holy Spirit, that we too may be a community of self-giving love, after your image.

We ask it in Jesus Christ's name
Amen.

CHILDREN AND ADULTS TOGETHER (2)

A CONTRIBUTION BY OREGINA BASIC CHRISTIAN COMMUNITY MEMBERS (ITALY) TO THE VISITING UK TEAM, 1983.

Q. Are you working on any particular issues at the moment?

A. A question we are concentrating on is how children can grow in faith. Within the community there have been several marriages and there are now children of these marriages aged from three to seven years. There have also been people joining the community who have older children. The adults met for one year without the children, to clarify their understanding of their responsibilities, and then met together with the children again. They took as a starting point the idea that Jesus had been sent to us by God, that he is a brother and friend to everyone and the Messenger of Peace. Every two weeks we discuss the high points of his life and seek to discover how these can be meaningful to the children. They in turn express their understanding of each high point of Jesus' life in mime, drawings, songs etc. They have found Christ to be a living and meaningful person who attracts them and produces concrete response in their lives. They give testimony to their faith.

However, the factor which has most impact on the children is not the method used but the witness of the lives of the parents themselves and of the whole community. The approach made with children contains within it the essence of our whole approach, which includes social criticism and criticism of our own adequacy in living the faith as a community. It is important for our children that they hold to values which are different from those which mark society today.

Q. How do you understand the ideas of 'Church' and 'theology'?

A. The Church is not a wonderful, perfect organization moving through history, but ordinary people trying to live the faith, seriously and in freedom. Our theology takes shape from the faith we live day to day. For the theology to be authentic, we have to be seen to live for the poor and not for the rich. The Church must be for the last and least.

* * *

PRAYER

God the Lord

Empty us that we might be filled even as Jesus Christ emptied himself that all your fullness might dwell in him.

We confess that we try to fit the biblical message into a framework which is acceptable to us, and that thus its challenge is blunted. We resist interpretations based on insights gained in cultures and contexts which are strange to us – though these could bring us alive to that new light which may continually spring forth from the Word. Empty us of such self-protection.

Give us ears to hear: 'The word of God is alive and active. It cuts more keenly than any two-edged sword, piercing so deeply that it divides soul and spirit, joints and marrow; it discriminates among the purposes and thoughts of the heart. Nothing in creation can hide from him; everything lies bare and exposed to the eyes of him to whom we must render account.' (Hebrews 4.12-13)

Bare us to the truth. Send us to do your will.

Empty us of the vanity which leads us to treat children merely as pre-adults, valuing their potential rather than their present qualities so that we divide them from the total community in which they should play a full part. Teach us how to provide an imaginative framework for their growth, that they might learn the positive contribution of discipline. Give us that readiness, which Jesus advocated, to sit at their feet and be taught the things of the Kingdom.

Save us from making our children in our image instead of freeing them to grow into the fullness of the life you have in mind for them.

Bare us to the truth. Send us to do your will.

Empty us of our preoccupation with the good name and the good fortune of the Church, for your eyes are on the world. Help us, as a Church, to be spent for those on whom you would have us lavish love. Set us in the midst of life, not in a protected place apart. May there be that in us which allows all your little ones to see, day by day, how precious they are in your sight: that they may lift their heads and reject the world's low valuation of their lives.

Bare us to the truth. Send us to do your will.

In Jesus Christ's name
Amen.

THE DISPLACED FIND FRIENDSHIP

Q. What is it like to be an immigrant, even from one part of one's country to a strange part?

A. You feel lost. Living in a city after being in a rural area, you find yourself lacking any of the familiar reference points to give you your bearings. People leave a place in which they are personally known to everyone and they come to a place of tower-blocks where they are unknowns. This simply means that they have to search for religious or cultural or political forms of meeting. They have real difficulty in working out what their faith means in the city and relating that to the way they learned it back home. In light of all this, those of us who believe that the Christian faith is crucial for our lives today have been coming together in small groups. We set out to rediscover the meaning of faith in this new context.

Q. Is there a gathering of such a group in your house each week?

A. This is the way it is. We are in a Christian community of fifty to sixty people. We divide ourselves into small groups of eight or ten. It is in small groups that we can really get deep with one another, especially in matters of faith. The small size of the group is quite essential – here we find it possible to share our deepest feelings, the things which really disturb us. The meetings last for two to three hours and take place once every two weeks.

We also meet to celebrate our faith on a weekly basis. The form of the gathering for celebration and reflection is fairly well fixed. We start with a reflection on some theological or pastoral theme which has preoccupied some of the groups. The theme will be made known beforehand to those who assemble and some material about it supplied. One group will be asked to do more work on it and to present it. What follows is a rich dialogue which clarifies understanding and action, and which will continue in discussion in the smaller groups. We finish with a Eucharist. The preparation of the Eucharist will be committed to selected people. It is a leisurely, spacious and festive gathering.

* * *

PRAYER

Pray for young people, migrants from home and family:

– those who have kicked over the traces, resenting and rejecting the home life which they have experienced;

– those who have been shown the door and are given no alternative;

– those whom death or accident have robbed of close relatives; who are uprooted and made into wanderers;

– those who have an instinct and liking for wandering;

that they might find in us friendship and support.

Pray for those hungry on the streets:

– those who sleep in doorways, and in boxes;

– those frozen through sleeping outdoors;

– those who search for work and know despair when they do not find it;

– those tempted to commit suicide;

that they might find in us friendship and support.

Pray for those who, at their wits end

– are tempted to turn to crime, and who give in;

– get into the hands of pimps and are prostituted;

– turn to drugs and get into the power of drug-dealers;

– drift into situations of violence and are fearful for life and limb;

that they might find in us friendship and support.

St James says, 'If a brother or sister is without clothing and in need of daily food, and one of you says to them, "Go in peace, be warmed and be filled" and yet you do not give them what is necessary materially, what use is that? Even so faith, by itself, if it does not find concrete expression, is dead.' (James 2.15)

How are friendship and support to be made real? Possible decisions:

– to fight against government actions which marginalize young people and to fight for policies which take account of the pressures they are under and of their needs;

– to support financially and in other ways statutory and voluntary bodies which meet young people arriving at bus and railway stations, who provide food and a place to stay;

– to support police and social workers who seek to alleviate the situation;

– to keep alert for signs of self-mutilation and suicide in the despairing.

THE CHURCH 'BORN FROM BELOW'

Q. How did the basic Christian communities start in the Basque country in general and in Vitoria in particular? Was it with priests or laity?

A. It was with an event – *the* event of 3 March 1976. There was a strike which went on for a month and involved the whole factory population of this area. It was during Franco's time. Trade-union activity was forbidden. But the workers got access to a church. The police threw in smoke bombs. When the people came out, five were killed by police fire. This was the impulse which really led to the development of basic Christian communities here. The bishop in the area did not respond in any Christian way to the killing of workmen, so those who had been angered by this event made up their minds they had to discover for themselves what the faith had to say to them.

Concerned people – quite a mixture of people – got together to develop the structures of pressure for justice. The fact that they were not acting merely politically but from the point of view of faith was something new, and raised questions. The initiative was essentially lay. Although there were those in the official Church who were sympathetic and supportive, the main authorities of the Church did not become involved. This movement had to take place outside the parishes which were lined up with the Church hierarchy.

To start with, all the groups had a priest attached to act as a co-ordinator and to be, in a certain way, a specialist in faith. Essentially, the b.c.c.s analysed the situation and then tried to work out what the Christian response should be. This process led to other, much wider, questions about life. These had not been open to them before. There was no intention of putting a distance between themselves and the official Church – they simply *were* the Church trying to live its life faithfully. Questions of divorce, abortion, the media and violence became matters that people no longer left to the authorities but tried to make sense of themselves. The official Church tried to call this movement a parallel Church, whereas it was simply Church. The gospel is more likely to make us fear the temptations of power than the possibilities of revolution!

* * *

THE ROLE OF CONFLICT IN SHALOM

'My own peace I give you,
a peace the world cannot give ...' (John 14.27)

> *Peace, you deceiver,*
> *giving*
> *all you profess:*
> *changing*
> *red-blooded human kin of God*
> *– mind, spirit, fire –*
> *to drowsing trees*
> *or chirping on their stems*
> *while suns swing by*
>
> *peace, you seducer*
> *luring*
> *from true spouse Christ*
> *saying*
> *'Teresa yes. Camilo, no!'*
> *– one part undone –*
> *'Piety, yes,*
> *home, job – a world that plain*
> *people can grasp'*
>
> *peace, you betrayer,*
> *sucking*
> *heat from the fight*
> *twisting*
> *to devil's own exegesis*
> *'love', 'promise', 'grace' –*
> *dealing in guile,*
> *the knave card 'Reconcile!'*
> *at Truth's straight flush:*
>
> *peace, you bright bastard, leave us*
> *that peace of Christ receive us.*

The partitions of Japanese houses can be removed to provide a substantial meeting place in even quite small houses. One Sunday morning, some forty or fifty people gathered in such a home. Most of them were young adults. Some Western hymns were sung and some of Japanese origin. The readings were followed intently, and people really worked on the exposition of four different Bible passages although they did not discuss the interpretation aloud with the young pastor. I did not need to know the language to be part of a vitalizing and refreshing act of worship.

'A pity about that,' said my guide as we left.

'A pity? Far from it! An exhilarating experience – even for a foreigner!'

'I mean, it's rather a pity that this Church grew as it did.'

'How did it grow then?'

'Well, one or two Christians moved into this area and discovered one another. They started to meet for Bible study and worship. Then the quality of their life began to attract others. Most of the people you saw there came from Shintoism, or some other faith, or no faith at all. It was the sheer quality of life of the original group which produced this Church.'

'But that is all good – what worries you?'

'Well, you see, the original group was simply the Church of this place, the Christians who happened to be here and who were drawn together by the common faith they were living out. But, unfortunately, they were all kinds: Roman Catholics, Baptists, Salvation Army, the lot.'

'But isn't that a good thing?'

'In one way. But, we have not only learned the gospel from you Westerners, we have received your divisions. The people who have joined this house-church cannot be baptized. There is no one tradition into which they all may enter. The Church cannot grow into its fullness.'

* * *

REFLECTION

The challenge to ecumenical advance today is being quite misread. It is so often represented as a search by the Churches for common ground on which they may stand and common fields in which they may co-operate. It is, rather, to be so engaged in bringing the world towards the purpose for which God created it that the risks are taken of the Church's being torn apart.

Christians will take different sides when they get into battles to change the present world into the order of God's promise. They will split the Church down the middle on how to handle different issues. The big ecumenical question is not whether they can develop more harmonious relationships. It is whether they have enough in Jesus Christ to hold them together against all the odds when they get engaged where it matters. Similarly, in direct relationships with one another, they must respect one another so deeply and sincerely that they can take one another to task about the beliefs and practices. It is a mistake to believe that Christians should be polite to one another. What they do owe to one another is courtesy. Courtesy has been an honourable word in the English language, at least as far back as Chaucer. It means having deep regard for other people – so deep that you are prepared to tell them openly and honestly what they need to know for their own good instead of glossing that over to smooth things out. The bond between Christians should allow for honest and open speech which is humble and yet unvarnished. So Jesus spoke. So Paul took Peter and the young Church to task. What mattered was the Kingdom.

The options are these:

– You have an unrenewed Church which is split apart and cannot function as the bearer of healing; a Church in which different denominations are drawn together on the understanding that awkward issues will not be raised. Unity becomes a security-device to preserve ongoing Church life. A Church at peace with itself in a world of disorder is a testimony against the gospel.

– You have a Church which is radically engaged in the struggles for a new world. A Church committed where it matters, prepared to be broken for the healing of the nations is a sign of hope and of ecumenical maturity.

Is not the sacrament which nourishes the Church in its ongoing life a sign that it is through brokenness that humanity might reach out to wholeness?

FORGIVENESS HEALS (1)

There was a young lass in Rosyth who was a bit wild but very like-able, and she was known as 'one for the boys'. She came to church quite often and her family was part of the congregation. One day she sought me out. She did not say what the problem was but I think it had to do with giving in to sexual advances which she might well have invited in the first place. She was an attractive, lively girl.

We met and she told me that something had happened in her life which meant that she wanted to ask God for forgiveness for things which she now felt ashamed about. She wanted a clean start. Would I, without probing any further, allow her to confess her sinfulness and pronounce over her God's absolution so that she could make the fresh beginning which she longed for?

At an agreed time we met in the vestry. I told her that, for an act of this kind, there needed to be a second element. Would she agree that I make a general confession in her presence of the sin which infected my life and that she pronounce God's forgiveness over me? Then I would hear her confession and pronounce God's forgiveness over her. She was startled. She had put me on a different plane. I had to get her to see that there is no category of people so good that all they need to do is to assure others of the forgiveness of God to release them from their sins. We ordained people are as human as they come. As we talked it through, she came to see my point.

We went into the front of the church. We heard one another's confessions. We declared God's forgiveness and absolution over one another. We rejoiced together. Both of us received a clean start.

* * *

'Do you know that your body is a temple of the Holy Spirit, who is in you, whom you have from God, and that you are not your own? For you have been bought with a price: therefore glorify God in your body.' (1 Corinthians 6.19-20)

PRAYER

Consider young people who become sexually mature, who know new powers and new yearnings. Let us pray that they may honour their bodies as gifts from God; not shy away from but welcome the new possibilities which maturity brings, and discover the freedom to remain in charge of what they do.

Think with understanding and sympathy of pressures on them to conform to the standards and tastes of their peer group and of the difficult test of coping with their continuing dependency on elders and balancing that with the need to find personal identity and assert independence.

Pray especially for those who have had no framework of family discipline against which to work out new freedoms; and those whose lives have been so tightly controlled that they are tempted either to conform tamely or rebel outrageously.

Pray for parents in the difficult task of helping young people through this stage. Pray for the Church that it may give young people space and voice, imaginative support, and uphold them by prayer and sensitive understanding.

Examine yourself concerning:

– your ability to delight in your sexuality, expressing it so that it is a blessing, not a curse to others;

– your ability to empathize with young people, giving them the space they need and still be someone they can turn to.

'Search me, O God, and know my heart, try me and know my thoughts; and see whether there is any wicked way in me: and lead me in the way everlasting.' (Psalm 139.23-24)

Amen.

A member of the kirk session in Rosyth, a lawyer, went missing. Several days later he was found unshaven, red-eyed. It came out that he had been embezzling money and the police had caught up with him. He was the kind of man whom you would not expect to take such a course. But there it was.

He was tried, sentenced, jailed. The first message I was able to convey to him gave him heart. The kirk session sent their greetings and said they wanted him to remain one of them. This touched him deeply. But he felt he could not comply and put in his resignation which they had to accept.

When he came out of jail, the lawyer and myself had, at his request, an act of mutual confession and absolution. But that was only a start. There was still the tough business of his rejoining the congregation. One of the problems was that among them were some who had lost money by his default. Officially, he had paid the penalty and was now cleared of responsibility towards them. The only job he was able to get was at a much lower rate of pay. But he wanted to make recompense as far as he could, and suggested to me a fairly sacrificial scheme for laying aside so much each week to reimburse those who were hardest hit by his defect. The hurdle of joining the congregation again and taking part in Sunday worship remained. Several times he ducked away from that fence at the last minute.

At last he plucked up courage to attend a service with his family. I saw him immediately afterwards and asked how it was. The tears came to his eyes. 'I wasn't cold-shouldered,' he said. 'Nor was I fussed over. It was just "Aye, Jim, glad you're back!"'

Ordinary folk may instinctively use 'faith-language' rather than religious language at crucial points, through an intuition for what is appropriate and which also has a gospel flavour to it. If members of the congregation had said, 'We forgive you,' this would have left them looking superior and left him feeling broken. As it was, they found words which naturally expressed their forgiving acceptance of him back into full fellowship.

* * *

'All have sinned and come short of the glory of God.'
(Romans 3.23)

PRAYER

Consider our tendency to link the idea of serious sin with what other people do, especially those who are found out and whose sin is made public. Remember the parable of the Last Judgement – when God judges the lives of people and nations the result is a turn-up for the books;

– and pray for those labelled 'bad lots', in light of the fact that all have sinned, but not all have been found out.

Think of the policies of those holding power which violate human beings, families, regions, nations, hemispheres; which deface the image of God in people wherever they are taught to bow their heads before injustice; and of violence which is a reaction to injustice and has in it the demand for a true order of society;

– and pray for those labelled 'trouble makers' when the trouble they cause is trouble God wants to see – trouble which leads to God's Kingdom being established on earth and fulfilled beyond.

Consider the way in which Churches tend to assimilate their thinking to the values of the age in which they live;

– and pray for the Church that it may be alert to establish Christ's new law of love, and promote the kind of order expressed in God's way of working established through the whole fabric of Creation.

Rejoice in communities of faith which break through traditional and stereotyped attitudes

– which are found alongside those who struggle and suffer, prepared to get a bad name for righteousness sake;

– which gladly accept back into their company those who have gone astray and find words of forgiveness which can restore to people the dignity and place they have in God's sight;

– which are so aware of themselves as forgiven sinners that no one is rejected by them.

To God be glory for ever
Amen.

SPINNING UNITY (1)

When, in 1960, Scottish Churches House came into being, Rev. Dr Archie Craig and I were invited to meet with representatives of the Aberdeen Churches to alert them to the potential of this new venture. The RC Bishop of Aberdeen wrote courteously to say that he could not take part in this meeting. He asked whether it might be possible for one of us to meet with him and with some of his people afterwards. I was deputed.

There was an encouraging gathering of priests and lay leaders from all parts of the diocese. We had an animated discussion about options now opening out for working in new relationship.

I had heard about the renovation of the cathedral. At the end of the gathering, the Bishop showed me over it and pointed out the changes. 'We have taken the table-altar to where the people are,' he said. 'Those who preside at the mass are now facing them, and are more clearly at one with them. We have cleared out all the religious clutter and re-stored a basic simplicity to the building,' he continued. Then, with a little smile and sideways glance: 'We are leaving religious clutter to you Protestants now!'

At the back was a side-chapel dedicated to Mary. 'Note what she has in her hand,' he observed. 'It is not a sceptre but a distaff. This is not the Queen of Heaven but the humble handmaid of the Lord.'

As we returned towards the entry, he said, 'Well, that's it, I take it.'

'No,' I replied.

'What else?'

'We haven't prayed for one another.'

Side by side, we knelt on hassocks. He prayed for new community and new venturing by the Churches in Scotland using the fresh base now available. We asked God to renew the whole Church in unity, truth and peace.

* * *

A HYMN OF THANKSGIVING FOR MARY

We praise you for the mother of our Lord
who lent her body for the Saviour's birth
despising like her Son the disrepute
the price to bring salvation to the earth:
      When called may we, like Mary answer still
      'Be it to us according to your will.'

Make ours the song that poured from Mary's heart
who saw a world renewed in all its sum,
the poor lifted high, the mighty ones dethroned
the hungry filled, the rich without a crumb:
      Enlisted for this fight we answer still
      'Be it to us according to your will.'

As Jesus' harshness, cutting to the quick,
placed human faith before all ties of kin;
just as a vine, submitted to the knife,
through pruning finds new fruitfulness begin:
      When pruned, may we like Mary answer still
      'Be it to us according to your will.'

Let us, like Mary standing by the Cross,
when all our hopes for life collapse in dust
be, there, embraced in new community
deep grounded not in fate but living trust:
      Bereft, may we like Mary answer still
      'Be it to us according to your will.'

As when the day of resurrection dawned
and Mary found new life and her reward –
so bodies, like a sacrifice prepared,
are needed that the world might know its Lord:
      May we, the called, like Mary answer still
      'Be it to us according to your will.'

SPINNING UNITY (2)

Scottish Churches House was brought into being as a house held by the co-operating Churches in Scotland as a common base for dialogue and initiatives. At that time Roman Catholics found it constitutionally impossible to take a formal part in that shared ownership but they were able to be in on everything informally from the earliest stage.

In regions of Scotland, the Roman Catholic/Protestant divide has been one which has seemed most intractable. In parts of the Highlands there has been respect and co-operation over centuries, but the south-west has experienced great bitterness and conflict. Accordingly, the Pope's visit in 1981 was looked forward to with some hope and some trepidation. Would he make things worse, or aid healing processes which were clearly under way? His direct answer was to extend an invitation to all Christians in Scotland to go on pilgrimage together, hand-in-hand.

During the visit he was presented with a beautifully wrought spinning wheel. He asked that it be, in turn, presented to Scottish Churches House, and thus to all Christians in Scotland. On the Eve of St Andrew's Day, Tuesday, 29 November 1983, the Apostolic Pro Nuncio, Archbishop Bruno Heim and Cardinal Gordon Gray presented the spinning wheel to the Very Rev. Prof. Robin A.S. Barbour, Chairman of the Scottish Churches Council, in the presence of representatives of the Churches. Robin Barbour accepted the gift as a sign of promise for the future and of longing for the time when the thread that is spun by the Churches in Scotland gets woven into one single garment, making visible their unity in Jesus Christ.

Thereafter, principals in the ceremony walked to the Chapel of the House where, in silent prayer together, they interceded for the unity in mission of the Churches in Scotland and for the work and witness and future service of Scottish Churches House. The vigil was maintained through the afternoon, evening, night and morning which followed.

* * *

'May God, the source of patience and encouragement enable you to have the same mind among yourselves, after Jesus Christ's example: so that, united in mind and voice, you may give glory to God, his Father.' (Romans 15.5-6)

REFLECTION

When it comes to establishing unity among the followers of Jesus Christ, the previous passage advocates 'patience'. The original text suggests the idea of holding on, keeping your head above water, surviving. Much of this occurs in our common use of the word 'patience'.

However, the biblical use has also a more positive flavour. It speaks of suffering accepted as a sacrificial means whereby life can be offered up to God who gave it. This results in a transformation of the human situation. (Have you noticed that the Suffering Servant story in Isaiah 53 is a success story?) In the New Testament, 'patience' carries with it an awareness that the essential work to transform human life has already been done in the life, death and resurrection of Jesus Christ. To gather the fruits of that mighty work in our human societies and Churches today demands patience:

– the realization that God is the great Doer, ours is but a share in the doing; so we are not to be anxious as we tackle our particular assignments, God is in charge of all life;

– persistence, whatever the odds stacked against us;

– expectation that our offering will be relevant and have significance for the establishing of the Kingdom; i.e. the whole fabric of created life pulsating to God's heart-beat.

We can do all things through Christ who strengthens us.

PRAYER

– for those who are alert to respond to Jesus Christ's prayer, 'Father, may they be one in us, as you are in me and I am in you, that the world may believe it was you who sent me' (John 17.21);

– for those who feel their security threatened should they move from set positions, and pull down the shutters of their minds;

– for those who reject superficial unity, insisting that deep problems be dealt with; and yet stay open to new light, ready for new paths;

Reflect on James 1.3-4: '... patience too has its practical results so that you will become fully developed, complete, with nothing missing.'

TRUE AUTHORITY

'You're going to meet a Pope, Ian Fraser,' I said to myself, 'so it's to be straight and firm and brotherly. He's no more important than the taxi-driver who took you here – though that's important enough in God's sight. No deference, then. Just courtesy.' A minute later, I searched a lively face, met twinkling eyes, received brotherly greetings and knew that the Pope of the Coptic Orthodox Church would have the profoundest respect for the maddest Cairo taxi-driver and would never think of himself as his superior. You felt at once that here was one who saw Christ in all kinds of people.

I had been warned that the Pope had a very full day, and that about ten minutes had been crammed into the programme for me. Our conversation sparked, lit fires of conviction, touched off answering vision and enthusiasm. 'That was one of the liveliest ten minutes I have spent in my life,' I said to my companion as we left. 'An *hour* and ten minutes,' he corrected. My watch insisted it was so. Pope Shenouda had quietly waved away others, unnoticed by me. What made time pass so quickly? Here was a man who, in his main conversation and in his asides, betrayed a sense of living in one world fellowship of faith. Here was a man who was ecumenical in a quite unforced, seemingly instinctive way. Here was one with a deep pastoral concern, so that you felt that he was blessing people by being with them without even raising his hands in blessing. A sharp, prophetic intellect allowed him to concentrate on the world's sores and shames and still keep a merry heart.

From this man, I took back some incisive words and insights. 'What have we a *right* to share? Theology and spirit, no more. If we also bring our culture, music, ways of life, architecture, that is imposition, a hindrance to the truth.' 'Renewal is like a seed. Forces outside itself must enable it to break the husk and begin to grow. But any help which is of the Spirit will empower it to sprout *as itself*.' 'Authority in the Church is a form of the practice of love, trust and simplicity. Discipline is an exercise in responsibility for the truth. In any gatherings of Christians, truth must preside, not status – then clergy and laity each exert their proper authority.'

* * *

PRAYER

Pray for those in positions of authority, tempted to exercise power in a 'rulers of the Gentiles' way which Jesus said was not to be our way; who, impregnated by the spirit of Jesus, may rather learn to handle responsibilities of high office with real humility;

– that, in Church or public life, they may be continually converted to the way of Jesus; and may receive that critical support from an imaginative community of faith which both keeps them from evil and frees them for good.

Pray for an understanding of authority which recognizes that it comes 'from above' (as Jesus said to Pilate), not a possession but a trust;

– that, in boardroom and classroom, on shop floor and in office, in government department and in the home, authority may not be an imposition but a form of responsibility and humble service which all concerned can acknowledge: that, thus, 'truth may preside, not status.'

Pray for those in public position who seem to be free but have to cope with forces at work which tie their hands and determine their way beyond their own choosing;

– that there may be others who take the trouble to understand, uphold them in prayer, and conspire with them to see how they may break out of bondage.

Pray for those who are tempted to work overmuch to justify their important positions, neglecting their bodies, their families and all that can make life rounded and complete;

– that they may achieve a balance, and get the gift of a merry heart.

Lord God Almighty,

We praise and bless you who are the final Authority over all life, for in that authority we can have confidence, in it we can rest.

We praise and bless you for those who, activated by the Holy Spirit, hold high responsibility and exercise it with grace and sensitivity.

Give us the courage to confront brute force masquerading as authority wherever it is found in Church or state, in industry or home, in school or office or hospital; that true accountability to you may mark the use of power and thus make it recognizable as genuine authority.

We ask it in Jesus Christ's name

Amen.

A COMMUNITY AT WORSHIP

In Oporto, Portugal, the service which mustered the small basic Christian communities in that area for a monthly celebration, lasted from 10a.m. to 5p.m. The first twenty minutes or so were spent in members hugging one another, exchanging greetings, and getting up to date with news. This was all part of the worship. The first hymn was one composed in the community. It was not only sung but danced. Bible readings followed. Then about an hour's sermon/reflection was built up from these. The small groups had met during the previous week and struggled to see how insights from the text could illuminate their life in the world. There was a mature interpretation.

In the early afternoon we shared a common meal – very much a feature of the worship of basic Christian communities. Mario, the worker-priest then prepared the Eucharist.

All this sounds too good to be true. But are these people 'spiritual athletes'? Anything but. Listen to them when, the bread broken and the wine poured out, they tell of their own brokenness and pour out their hearts in union with the bread and wine. You will hear of frustration and failure in relationships affecting husbands, wives, young people, parents. You will be told of illnesses and despondencies. There will be word of humiliations and stresses at work, in searching for work, in looking for alternative work. 'Cast down, but not destroyed' – the words come instinctively to mind.

The theme for the day is 'How are we to live the joy of our faith?' Sorrows once shared, testimonies are made to a power which overcomes in and through suffering. Isabel, tears streaming down her cheeks from the remembered vexation of being blamed by her employers for taking a week off work to calm a suspected ulcer on doctor's orders, brightens. Her face becomes sun shining through rain. She ends, with quiet firmness, 'We fight on.' (She died of cancer within a year.)

Members of the community do not depart until they have consolidated plans for the political and social engagements to which faith directs them. Some of these they will fulfil together, some separately.

* * *

REFLECTION

Mario as the worker-priest in the Oporto community of small communities is not prominent in the day-to-day leadership, which principally lies in the hands of women. This is quite often the case in basic Christian communities. In them, women are not artificially denied the exercise of leadership gifts as so often happens in traditional Churches. The ordained become a modest presence, an at-the-side, enabling, not dominating, presence – a sign for the whole Church of what ordination should mean.

When Jesus was challenged on divorce, he pointed to foundational teaching in the first chapters of Genesis which not only contradicted current divorce legislation but challenged the practice of that time which devalued women. In the Genesis account it is women and men together who are created in the image or likeness of God, in partnership given charge of the development of the earth. If one rather than the other is reckoned to be the crown of Creation, it is woman (chapter 2). She is the end and goal of the whole process. She is created out of human matter whereas the man is created out of earth stuff (but the 'rib' again suggests, as in chapter 1, a side-by-side relationship). In chapter 3, a mark of the fall from grace is the domination of man over woman. The requirement that genuine partnership between women and men be re-established was what Jesus brought to light.

PRAYER

Praise God for this wonderful Creation and for the trust placed in women and men to manage it together.

Confess, for human society and especially for the Church, ways in which the radical basis of life has been usurped by the domination of men over women; and confess any sin of this for which you are personally responsible.

Promise amendment of life – in relationships, and in fighting for a more just and true ordering of life in Church and in society.

To God's greater glory
Amen.

ORDINATION: EVEN FOR MEN?

With Honduran companions, I had travelled to the southern border-
lands of Honduras over roads whose construction and quality under-
lined the USA's intention to put maximum military pressure on the
government of Nicaragua. We arrived in the Choluteca district. On
one side were refugees who had escaped the killing fields of El Salvador. On the other were the Contras.

The small outpost had a room large enough for fifty or sixty people. They turned up in twos or threes. There was an earth floor. Hens
angled their heads to size up the risks and, with many starts and flus-
ters, managed to get a few pickings among the feet. Pigs nosed in at
the door, intelligently deciding that feet meant kicks and ventured no
further. The hens' want of intelligence clearly made them the gainers.

Eventually the service started and was enthusiastically carried
through by leaders and participants. The *delegada de la palabra* (delegate of the Word), the assistant *delegada* and the catechist (who was
responsible for teaching the children) were all women. Afterwards
they told me of the training they received, one session per month, in a
town within reasonable distance. People were thus not withdrawn
from involvement in their local communities but, over a period of
time, were resourced and built up for the leadership to which the
Church had appointed them in these communities.

I asked whether men were also trained in the same way, at the
same centre. The question seemed to produce confusion and perplexity. 'Think of the nature of the work. It consists basically of exposition of the Scriptures and pastoral care.'

'So?'

'Well, men and women have different gifts for different types of work.
It is not that we push the men aside or think less of them – you saw
how many of them were in the congregation. It's just that they and we
are suited for different tasks. I mean – for scriptural exposition and
pastoral care, it wouldn't be natural to turn to men, would it? It's not
their kind of thing, is it?'

＊ ＊ ＊

REFLECTION

'They have stolen our names,' say women ruefully, thinking of evidences in Scripture of women's crucial part in the work of salvation, which have been played down through the centuries.

The patriarchs have been given prominence. But they had to wait on their wives for unusual, delayed births before the line of promise could be established. The saving work of the exodus was not initiated by Moses at the burning bush but by an all-woman operation involving midwives, a mother and sister, a princess and her train – without them there would have been no Moses. It was through Mary's offering of herself that Christ came; through women's voices that the resurrection was first announced. At so many of the generative points of the history of salvation, it was women who were agents of liberation.

Confess any of the following:

– failures to do justice to the partnership God established;

– despising of one sex or the other or of people sexually untypical;

– support for government policies which discriminate or fail to counter discrimination;

– any failure to take up the cudgels to right wrongs.

Pray for

– women still severely handicapped as a result of custom and tradition;

– women whose work in the home is given low esteem;

– women denied access to education and public life;

– women who are afraid to break free of oppression.

Rejoice in

– women who, through the gospel, demand new voice and place in society and Church, who lift up their heads and see salvation drawing nigh;

– who call on all peoples to receive as a gift from God new relationships of mutual respect and trust; that God's promise for the earth might be fulfilled and all flesh see it together.

Amen.

UNPRETENTIOUS AUTHORITY

INTERVIEW WITH FR DANIEL JENSEN OF MARYKNOLL, GUATEMALA

Q. How do you see the current situation in your country?

A. What's happening, I believe, is that the Indians and other rural people are becoming aware of their Christian responsibility and are growing to Christian maturity. They realize that they have a job to do as Christians here in the world. The fact that they protest their poverty, and the fact that they are now recognizing that this gruesome life which kills off their children is not the will of God is being seen as a threat to the whole status quo of the country. Basic Christian communities are an anathema to the people who don't want to see that status quo changed.

Q. Is there a tendency for the powers that be, then, to identify the leaders of basic Christian communities and try and get rid of them? Are they suffering particularly?

A. In the international press you'll hear about the priests and sisters who are being massacred here in Guatemala, but you rarely ever hear of the catechists who have disappeared – and most of the catechists are leaders of the basic Christian communities. I don't think we could even begin to count the number of catechists who have had to pay the supreme sacrifice. But the fact that they have given their lives is, to me, a sign that they have become fully aware of their own Christian identity and their own role as leaders within the Christian community.

Q. Does it not tend to be a self-defeating kind of thing, this policy of assassination? God raises up the most unlikely people to fill spaces left by previous leadership!

A. That's true. Another thing is that, in Indian culture, the person you least suspect to be the leader, really is. It's very hard to tell, in an Indian community, exactly who the leader is. It might be the dirty little old man who's sitting over in the corner. But the community itself recognizes where the leadership comes from.

* * *

Jesus said of the shepherd: 'the sheep follow him because they know his voice; and a stranger they will not follow, for they know not the voice of strangers.' (John 10.5)

REFLECTION

Jesus did not belong to any authority structure. He spoke with authority, not as the scribes. Officers sent to apprehend him returned empty-handed choosing to face the ire of their own authorities rather than to contest his authority (John 7.44-47). When challenged by the chief priests and elders, he threw the challenge back upon them.

John the Baptist did not belong to an authority structure either. Did they recognize in his baptizing mission an authentic exercise of authority? They had no answer. When Pilate, with Jesus before him, spoke of his own power as if it, of itself, were a form of authority, Jesus asked him to recognize that authority is not a possession and right given through human appointment but is given 'from above', designed to express the mind of Another.

Pray for those given positions of leadership in Church and society that they may see themselves as servants of God's large enterprise for Creation and not be full of themselves, trusting in their own power.

Remember .... and .... and .... called to exercise high responsibility.

Pray for those exposed to hostility, whether justified or not, for the way in which they handle the demands of high office – that they may repent of faults and persist in goodness even where their action may threaten vested interests, remembering .... and .... and .... who are under attack.

Pray for emerging leadership which carries its own authority. May those who are called not make their inadequacy a reason for refusing to lead but trust God to make up what is lacking in them; and that people may be given ears to recognize the voice of true leadership.

MINISTRY

A TESTIMONY OF THE SAN MIGUELITO COMMUNITY, PANAMA, 1972

'We find people taking on themselves a ministry based on what has been their own personal experience of resurrection in a particular area of their life.

'For instance, Fidel Gonzales is extremely adept at talking to people who are sick and dying, who need someone to put an element of hope in their lives. Fidel is good at this because he himself has twice been close to death. A car turned over and he was almost killed. His brain was badly damaged; one side was knocked out and the doctors thought he wouldn't be able to speak. However, he is left-handed, and he came out of it. It was an experience of resurrection for him. Slowly he learned to walk again, to write again. To hear him talk about his own experience, or talk to a person about what sickness implies, what death and the resurrection mean, is a fantastic experience because it is something that he has lived. He can fulfil ministry in this particular way.

'Favio and Adelina are a couple who have lived out the difficulties of marriage. This is a second marriage for Adelina. The first was an absolute disaster. To find in a marriage relationship what she has found with Favio! Then to see what Favio has become! Here is a man who stutters badly, and all of a sudden there he is, standing up and performing a liturgy of the Word, giving communion to an area group! This all comes out of the reality of resurrection in marriage, resurrection in a portion of life which they have lived out together. Hear Favio talk to a young couple who are going to be married – this man who really couldn't speak before: "Now look, marriage is a completely different experience, nobody can tell you what it is going to be like. It is going to be yours. You must put the elements of creativity in it." To listen to him speak to those about to be married is something to live for!

'You find people who have a clear vision of where we should be going. Chado is recognized not only in San Miguelito but by the laymen in all Panama as the person they most want to listen to, to tell their troubles to, and to have him say where we are all going. He has a tendency to shy away from this, he is afraid of this kind of power. But if there is a man with the ability and the vision to be a bishop in Panama, he is the one.'

* * *

SELF-EXAMINATION

In my own Church we at times speak carelessly of 'the ministry' referring only to that small part which is ordained. The Roman Catholic Church uses the word 'vocation' referring merely to a calling to the ordained priesthood. These ways of speaking conceal the reality that the only ministry or priesthood which is united to Jesus Christ's definitive ministry or priesthood is that of the whole people of God. All who are baptized are by that fact given gifts for ministry and called to employ them.

– Am I guilty of careless talk and careless thought which prevents all kinds of ordinary people from realizing that they share in Jesus Christ's ministry?

When the Church speaks more accurately of the ministry of the whole people of God, its practice may still lag far behind. It demands self-restraint on the part of traditional leaders to hold back. It demands patience and perseverance to encourage the whole body of people to share significantly in worship and witness. It also demands confidence-building techniques to release people to undertake responsibilities which had not been asked of them previously and to encourage them to see that they can draw on abilities which had been latent.

– Am I inhibiting the ministry of people endowed with the gifts of the Spirit?

– Am I myself prepared to play a fuller part in the whole Church's ministry?

Sometimes people are directly gifted for tasks. Sometimes they seem to develop abilities 'on the road'. Sometimes it is some severe testing which fits them to serve others who are destined to go through similar trials.

– Do I encourage those who have endured some form of hardship to see that this gives them gifts for ministry to others?

When, in the world at large, basic Christian communities have their leadership killed off by the military or the police, fresh leadership comes forward, often from the most unlikely quarters. God raises up people whom we would tend to overlook.

– Am I alert to see in people potential for ministry which can be only too easily overlooked?

Bishops may turn out to be theologically 'illiterate', while illiterates can get to the theological nub. Is not God's chief concern the destiny of his people?

In Brussels, Margaret and I met a Solima nun who worked in Pueblo Joven, Brazil. She told us, 'There are very poor people there. There is no water, there is no light, it is terrible. We had to return there because the bishop did not want to renew the contract with us.

'One of the things which he said was: "You are no longer involved in the things that are holy." I told this to one of the women of Pueblo Joven. She was very angry. She said, "For the bishop what is holy is all that is happening inside his Church. For me what is holy is the future of my people."

'The Saturday before Easter I came back to my convent. It's a big convent. They had the celebration of Easter with water, light etc. There is a priest in the convent who is a very artistic man. In the Chapel there was a beautiful scene, beautiful vestments, water, a very beautiful lighted candle and beautiful music. I came from Pueblo Joven where there was no water or light. I left the chapel and afterwards I said, "This is the degeneration of the liturgy."'

* * *

REFLECTION

Think with shame of the way in which some can get absorbed in the routine of Church ritual and liturgy so that immaculate observance becomes more important than the purpose for which the ritual was designed. Pray for those enmeshed in such preoccupations that they may be led to recognize their idolatrous nature, and repent and seek God's face anew.

– Let us all repent of empty observances in which we indulge.

Think with shame of worship which alienates the poor and the stranger, hiding from them God's welcoming face, God's open arms, God's longing that they know him. Pray for those who shut the door of the Kingdom of Heaven and neither go in themselves nor allow those who are going in to enter, that they may learn of Christ and be converted.

– Let us all repent of practices which exclude the poor and the stranger.

Think with shame of festivals so prepared as to give aesthetic pleasure to the privileged which thus exclude the poor. Pray for all who prepare celebrations that the telling power of the gospel and the grace of the human response may be woven in a seamless robe which allows all kinds of people to participate with meaning.

– Let us all repent of our inability to appreciate unfamiliar rhythms and styles of life which should find expression in worship.

Think with shame of Church leaders so theologically 'illiterate' that they think that it is what happens in Church buildings that matters to God. Pray that they may be taught by the theologically 'literate' that God's heart is set on the destiny of his folk.

– Let us all repent of superficial, Church-bound thinking.

Rejoice that, whether it occurs through ecclesiastical short-sightedness or ecclesiastical vision, so many faithful and imaginative Church workers are located where it matters, as were the perceptive nuns in Pueblo Joven.

Rejoice that those who make no pretension to intellectual ability and have no capacity for scholarship can have profound theological insights to share.

When the World Bank held a conference in Manila in 1976, squatters were displaced. They huddled under makeshift shelters, the children's teeth chattering in the rain. World Banks do not ask about the cost of their visiting. Free paint had been given out so that the appearance of things might be temporarily improved along the routes that cars would traverse.

In 1982, Margaret accompanied me to the Philippines. It was her first visit. We saw one of the effects of holding the SE Asian Games in that country at that time. We were in an area which was deemed to be an eyesore by the authorities. It would disgrace the country if competitors from many nations saw it. So, although the tenants had a legal right to their property and could not be faulted on payment of dues, bulldozers were sent in and their shacks demolished.

Residents were dumped on the outskirts of Manila, including a husband, wife and five children. They had no resources. No work was to be found. They drifted back. The husband, worn out by malnutrition and worry, coughed up his life-blood. There was no money to bury him. The body was put in a plastic bag and lay around for two weeks. Neighbours at last sacrificially raised enough to secure his burial.

The neighbours then built a lean-to against a wall and covered the framework with plastic (from the bag used for the body) to provide minimal accommodation for the widow and children. Its total extent was about 10' by 4'. A low platform kept the family off the mud and had to serve for beds. Five plastic bags acted as wardrobes for the children's clothes. That had to be home.

When a small boy gently took Margaret's hand and pressed it to his brow, seeking in this way her blessing, she felt all broken up. We felt we should be on our knees before these neighbours, seeking their blessing.

* * *

REFLECTION

'Power' (dynamis) is the ability to get things done. It depends on clout – on physical, psychological and other pressures brought to bear to get one's way. There need be no relationship to justice and truth; just to muscle.

'Authority' (exousia) points to a mandate given from beyond oneself to carry out the legitimate requirements of Another. It does not depend on clout but on the character of that person or organization, and the justice and truthfulness of his/her/its requirements. (World organizations, dictators, governments of many hues – take note.)

Pray for
– those who exercise power over others;
– those who are taken up with their status in the world's eyes, that they fail to appreciate the low esteem which others have to endure;
– those who use their power so to accumulate possessions, that others are deprived of life's basic necessities;
– those who use their power to determine what is good for other people, giving them no voice in decisions concerning their own future;
– those who will be brought face to face with God the Lord at the end of their days to account for their stewardship.

Give thanks for those who exercise power over others:
– who put power at the service of God's loving purposes;
– who, where power could be used unfairly to their own advantage, refuse to seek gain for themselves;
– who listen to others;
– who are prepared to be instructed by realities;
– who will be brought face to face with God the Lord at the end of their days to account for their stewardship.

Pray for those who speak and act with authority but have no back-up muscle:
– that they may not succumb to pressures to turn to mere power to get their way.

Meditate on Jesus' way of exercising power set out in Philippians 2.5-11.

In Rosyth, in 1948, Margaret and I had come to a church which had reached a position of considerable breakdown. A breakaway congregation met in the Co-op. hall. Kindly people had been drafted into offices in the church just to keep things going, even though they lacked appropriate gifts.

After some months it became clear to me that we could not develop the congregation's life of faith unless there was a drastic change in personnel, including Session Clerk, Chairman of the Congregational Board, Sunday School Superintendent, President of the Women's Guild, Church Officer and the organist. I talked about this with elders and others. It was an evaluation of the situation which many responsible people in the congregation shared. There had to be change if the church was to grow.

I decided on a direct approach. After much prayer, in fear and trembling, I would go to each house, pause at the gate, and force my legs to walk towards the door, stretch up and knock on the knocker – and then I knew I was for it! Whatever lay behind that door, I had no escape! My approach was consistent. I acknowledged the worth of each person and the graciousness they had shown by their readiness to fill a vacancy when the congregation was in difficulty. I told them they had important gifts, but they were not matched to their current work. A time of opportunity lay ahead. 'In the bowels of Christ,' would they be prepared to resign their office and leave it to us to find who should fill it, and invest their gifts in some other part of the congregation's life?

I do not know whether they were taken aback by an approach which combined bluntness with an appreciation of their readiness to help. At any rate they all handed in their resignations and all remained active members of the congregation.

* * *

'When Cephas came to Antioch, however, I opposed him to his face, since he was manifestly in the wrong. His custom had been to eat with the pagans but after certain friends of James arrived he stopped doing this and kept away from them for fear of the group that insisted on circumcision.'
(Galatians 2.11-12)

REFLECTION

Reflect on the need to get tough with one another in the Church as Paul did with Peter. It is the Church of Jesus Christ, but as an organization and as particular members it is subject to all the pressures that flesh is heir to. It always needs putting right. Jesus saw that we espy the mote in a neighbour's eye and miss the beam in our own. So any evaluations must not be simply personal but tested in community. In the testing we must be ready to discover that it is our judgements, not those of others, which are at fault, and that we are called to amend our lives.

We are constantly side-tracked by politeness and by a distaste for causing disturbance. We give these reactions honourable titles, calling the dodging of issues which need to be faced expressions of love and care for others. Jesus told his disciples straight what they were in for if they stayed with him. Some decided enough was enough and walked no more with him. The Kingdom depends on righteous living – relationships and lifestyles put right way up. So we have to be tough with one another for God's sake. Where some are in ill-fitting appointments it is neither good for themselves that things stay as they are, nor is it good for the Church and Kingdom. They can be relocated to where their gifts and energies find fruitful outlet.

The Church is given to be a sign, instrument and foretaste of the Kingdom of God. It is to be a pointer to the reality that God is in charge of all life. It is to be a means whereby that reality is given expression in the way we go about life here and now. It is to have a flavour of God's grace about it, making that Kingdom longed for by all kinds of people.

To leave the Church's sins, faults and inadequacies unchallenged is to let God and humanity down.

But it is tough to take one another to task for righteousness sake!

In September 1991, in Brno, Slovakia, I shared in a gathering of East European Christians who were meeting to consider their calling under Communist regimes. The group had met over the course of two decades despite restrictions on religious organizations and travel.

The following quiet testimony was given. In an area of open-cast coal mining in the old DDR electricity generating had developed. Steam-powered industries then took advantage of cheap electricity. The air was filled with dust and fumes. More and more land was taken over for industrial expansion. The local church was bulldozed. People were made refugees, their houses demolished in the advance. Even the graveyards were threatened.

Local Church people came together to see what faith demanded in the situation. First the members and the pastor undertook 'Samaritan' work, comforting and counselling the newly unemployed farmers who lost their fields, those compelled to move to new areas, and the old who thought that they would not be allowed to rest peacefully in their graves. They asked, 'Is the disturbance to our community justified?' They started to question government officials on energy priorities. Seeing the need to be more constructive, they examined alternatives to existing policies. Electricity was so cheap that it was being used wastefully, so they looked at ways energy could be used more economically which would make expansion unnecessary. The pastor became so expert in energy matters that he was treated as a specialist consultant by government officials.

During this time they reread their Bibles, discovering insights into the kind of economic priorities which might express God's way for human life; into the nature of the trusteeship of the planet which God had bestowed on human beings; into the concern for the well-being of their children's children which God required. Their action sparked off ideas, debate and action in the community, made industrial chiefs revise their plans, and proclaimed God's will that his beloved people had a right to share in decisions which shaped their destinies.

It was still no straightforward matter. If jobs in one field were lost through the expansion of a group of industries, jobs in another were lost by their contraction.

* * *

'The folly of God is wiser than human wisdom and the weakness of God stronger than human strength. My friends, think what sort of people you are whom God has called. Few of you are wise by any human standard, few powerful or of noble birth. Yet, to shame the wise, God has chosen what the world counts folly, and to shame what is strong, God has chosen what the world counts weakness. He has chosen things without rank or standing in the world to overthrow the existing order.'
(1 Corinthians 1.25-28)

PRAYER

Lord God, we give thanks:

– that the story of Noah and the flood affirms your intention to continue with human beings in all their sinfulness, instead of making a fresh start with creatures designed to conform tamely and unquestioningly;

– that the story of Exodus affirms your determination to free your people from bondage, however inclined they might be afterwards to turn against you to the lure of flesh-pots or the golden calf;

– that the story of the Exile and the Return affirms your willingness to temper your people through suffering, and to call them afresh to be pilgrims with you throughout history;

– that the story of the Incarnation affirms your sacrificial love in Jesus Christ, directed to the exodus of humanity from every kind of slavery;

– that the story of the local Church challenging the power industry affirms your willingness to work with poor material to achieve the pulling down strongholds, since transcendent power does not come from us but is yours alone.

It is not because of what we are that we offer ourselves to you, but because of what you can make of us.

It is not because of its quality that we offer the local Church to you, but because you can do exceeding abundantly above all that we ask or think.

It is not because of the world's deserving that we offer it to you, but because you have resources for its healing which can transform life.

Accept us, accept your Church, accept your world.

We ask it in Jesus Christ
Amen.

Among the lowly one finds a capacity to discern priorities with a simplicity which may look naïve, but which comes from concentrating on certain luminous and central things, paying attention to them as if they were jewels with many facets and fires, and letting other things fall into the background.

For a little while, I was the guest of a woman who lived in a poor quarter of San José, Costa Rica. She had little education, and her home, like all the houses around, was sub-standard and tiny for the eleven members of her family who lived there. Her husband left at five in the morning each day and worked until seven at night selling vegetables to support the family. They both belonged to a neighbourhood group which tried to see how changes which were needed in the area could be brought about.

One morning the woman was chatting with her friend. She said that the whole community must be roused to press for a fairer deal. Her friend protested that this was rather the responsibility of the local government officials. The tone sharpened:

'Do you believe in Jesus Christ?'

'Yes'

'Do you think Jesus Christ came to change life so that it was more the kind of life God wanted to see, or to leave it as it is?'

'I suppose to change it. Yes, to change it.'

'Do you think Jesus Christ meant to change life by himself, or did he mean us to share the work with him?'

(*Hesitantly*) 'I know he meant us to play a part.'

'Then how can you believe in Jesus Christ and let things stay as they are?'

* * *

REFLECTION

We are called to a fundamental recognition that God knows what is 'for us' in life. We do not get that insight from our own measurement of our abilities nor from the judgement of the wise on our potential. We get it by sharing life with the One who knows what all life is for. This gives us freedom. What we would like to be and do might fly in face of what we are made for. It might be the way to lose life, not find it. We are cut out to play a part in God's comprehensive purpose.

It is in Jesus Christ that we can see our true quality and calling – we are invited by God the Lord to be partners in transforming life so that it bears hallmarks of justice, truth and peace. To do that we need to recognize both our limitations and the freedoms conferred on us, both what is our responsibility and what is beyond us. Once our power is united with Christ's, fruitful action becomes possible. In union with him a new world beckons. We can set up signs of it right where we are.

PRAYER

Do I acknowledge what is beyond my power?

– Save me from worrying about or from grasping after what is not 'for me', I pray.

Do I acknowledge Christ's mission to change life?

– Save me from being content with things as they are, I pray.

Do I acknowledge that I am called to share in that mission?

– Save me from wasting talents and energy which should be spent on the part assigned to me, I pray.

Teach me your ways, O Lord. Lead me in your truth and teach me, for you are the God of my salvation.

Amen.

Nova Huta, near Cracow, is a steel city. About 120,000 people lived there in the 1970s when I first came in contact with it. The inhabitants had sent a delegation to the Communist Town Council and requested that five churches be built there to meet their needs. They were told that there were far too many churches already in Poland and that they would get no more. They went back several times, pressing their case. Each time they were rebuffed. Finally, they erected a cross on Church ground and over a period staged a vigil round it. I was told that six or seven people had been killed in the struggles with authorities around that area.

Eventually, the persistence of the people wore down the local Council who told them: 'You can have one church building. You will have to build it yourselves!' Such was the blindness of authorities! A building which people built themselves would be much more significant than a building built for them!

The church was built for 5,000 people, and 6,000 people piled in for each of the Sunday services. The authorities had specified no limits on size and so the people built the church of their dreams.

I visited the city again when the church was being built. The priest was labouring away with the others. The finished drawings suggested to me a ship of humanity sailing towards the future with all God's people in her hold.

When the church was finished it contained a large hall. This had come about in the following way. The people had gone back to the Council again and again with the complaint that damp was getting through the floor of the church and they needed an air-space under it. Once again they were refused. Once again they wore the Council down: 'Oh have your air-space!' they said. My informant told me, 'We just happened to make it large enough for 1,000 people. They did not prescribe any measurements!'

The God of Jacob, the twister, is still blessedly with us.

* * *

REFLECTION

The God whom we find in the Old Testament prefigures Jesus Christ in his ways with human beings.

When Moses protested: 'They (the sons of Israel) may say to me, "What is his (God's) name?," what then shall I say to them?' The response came 'I am who I am' or 'I will be who I will be' (the sense of personal existence is dynamic not static in Hebrew thought). I believe this means: 'You will find who I am if you travel with me, not if you stay where you are.'

God was also made known as the God of Abraham, Isaac and Jacob – that is, God was revealed through different forms of obedience concretely expressed in human lives:

– in Abraham, the risk-taker who with his household, went out not knowing where he would end up – a sign for faith's venturing;

– in Isaac, traumatized by seeing his father's knife poised over him, who opted for a quiet life thereafter – he dug wells and, when they were disputed, moved on, dug more wells and made a whole area fertile – a sign of the calling to non-violent persistence;

– in Jacob, who tricked his brother out of his birthright and blessing and outsmarted a crafty father-in-law – a sign of the astuteness which children of light should show to outfox children of darkness. (see Luke 16.1-8)

These patriarchs do not stand alone. We need new eyes and ears better to appreciate the notable part played in the history of salvation by Sarah, Rebekah and Rachel, long barren but essential generators of that promised line. They represent undervalued people who play an essential part in God's purpose.

ABASING AND HONOURING

In 1977, on a visit to the Philippines, I visited a housing project built at the direction of the First Lady, Imelda Marcos. The houses seemed pleasant. There was space for children to play and people to meet. But the way I heard the project described was 'alternative demolition'.

In reality, the poor were denied title to land on which to build their own homes. Instead their houses were demolished. A fraction of the dispossessed were rehoused in the First Lady scheme. Since the rents were too high for the people, they would live there for a month or two and then have to leave. They are made homeless by having houses provided for them above their means, every bit as much as made homeless by bulldozers.

I spent four days with gypsies in the Southeast of England on their shining new site.

It would soon get tatty if animals were around so animals were banned although they were part of the gypsies' life.

The authorities had used a points system to produce what they thought would be a just allocation, and to decide where each gypsy should live on the site. On traditional sites the importance of the extended family is obvious. Grandma might be in the caravan next door, a son and his wife on the other side, a brother across the way, and so on. The points scheme made no allowance for this. You might be at the back of the encampment, your brother near the entrance, and grandma away on the far side.

On the very fringe of the site, there was a park for lorries. The gypsies' main continuous trade was in scrap metal and any gypsy will tell you that if he has been collecting scrap all day, the only safe place to leave it at night before it can be sorted out and disposed of, is right under his window. No such option existed.

This scheme originated in a genuine concern of the responsible authorities for gypsy families. They did what they thought was good for them but they did not consult the gypsies themselves.

* * *

REFLECTION

In South African Bantustan, in 1970, the archdeacon of a community of people, who had been forcibly expelled from their homes and left to start again from scratch in the veldt, became convinced that they needed a medical clinic. He knew a European source which could be approached to provide money but he did not tap it. Instead, as he moved among his people, he raised questions about their health and the health of their children in the course of normal conversation.

For a year nothing happened. Then a few people came to him and said that they, the people of the township, felt that the medical care provided for them was inadequate. They would like to see what could be done to improve it. The archdeacon suggested they might discuss it with the elders, and this was agreed. The elders reacted positively, and a meeting was arranged with the chief. The outcome was common agreement that a medical clinic was needed and should be established.

But how could an idea become a reality? The people themselves volunteered to start a common fund, producing articles for sale, growing a few extra vegetables. The women had difficulty in getting a bare living from their small pieces of land with the men away at work but they still managed to grow a little extra. Two and a half years after the idea started, they had raised about $100, a significant amount considering the low level of income. Whatever was done from that point, even if outside money came in to meet the main part of the cost, the clinic would be something which belonged to the people.

There was still a price to pay. In the years it took to get the people to come to a common mind and get the clinic under way, those who might have been treated suffered ill health. On the other hand, once the community discovered its needs and its own power, it went from strength to strength. Before the clinic was even built, people were already examining possibilities of getting a better return from the land by using the services of the agricultural adviser more effectively. They felt stronger because power was left in their own hands.

PEOPLE COMING TO STATURE

THE PHILIPPINES, 1971

Cardinal Santos, then Cardinal-Archbishop of Manila, who had previously paid little attention to the Tondo squatter community's plea for help in getting land rights, was placed in an embarrassing position by Pope Paul VI's visit and his sympathetic reaction to the people's needs. Not long afterwards, the Cardinal unilaterally announced a large-scale housing project for the area. ZOTO – Zone One Tondo Organization, the squatter enterprise in Manila – denounced this as 'another traditional charity-oriented programme, ignoring the expressed wishes of the people and their right to participate in planning their own future.' They went to the 'open house' which the Cardinal traditionally held on Christmas Day to draw attention to their need. They carried bags of soil – if the Cardinal was to go ahead with *his* housing scheme, he would need earth on which to build it! – and demanded, among other things, that he support as an alternative the establishment of a ZOTO non-profit-making housing corporation.

In spite of the Government's promises that it would devote any vacant land which might be available to rehouse people displaced by port development, it began to build a warehouse on a vacant piece of ground known as Parola Compound. ZOTO swung into action, allotting space to families who were to start building their shacks, thus pinning out and claiming the disputed site. The people had just raised frameworks when the police appeared. They stopped, frightened. Believing that the will of the people needed strengthening, the ecumenical support team threw down a challenge. They told the people they would withdraw support if they didn't continue building by a certain deadline. There was hot debate, but no further action. The wisdom of the ecumenical team was confirmed when the government moved in and easily cleared the ground of the flimsy frameworks.

But then a delegation from ZOTO went to meet the team. They told them, 'You may have been right in the advice you gave us, but you put pressure on us to meet a deadline you chose. It is not *your* future, it is not *your* homes which are at stake, but ours. We would rather make bad decisions which we have come to in our own way and in our own time than accept good decisions which have been made for us. We will take responsibility for our own future.'

* * *

*Jesus observed that rulers of the Gentiles liked to be called
'Benefactors', and urged his disciples not to copy them.
(Luke 22.25-26)*

REFLECTION

*If we do good, we often want extra credit for it. Our giving may simply
come from an undeserved abundance of wealth or be a device to
minister to our self-esteem. We are undeserving servants. When we
have done all we can, we have only done our duty. (Luke 17.10) All our
gifts and resources come from God.*

*Pray for those in positions of power: that what they do well they may do
humbly.*

*The psalmist wrote: 'The earth is the Lord's and the fullness thereof, the
world and all its people' (Ps. 24.1) and 'The heavens are yours, the
earth also: the world and all that it contains.' (Ps. 89.11) Since a
feature of human sin is the determination to hang on to possessions as
if they were ours by right, pressure must be brought to bear to secure a
fairer distribution of resources which God owns and has given for all
to enjoy. Belief in God may lead to land-invasions!*

*Pray for those with great possessions that they may recognize that God's
final right of ownership is final, and be prepared, as was Zaccheus, to
redistribute their goods.*

*Pray for those denied even a basis for living, that their conviction that
God's provision is for all may lead them to fight for fairer shares for
everyone.*

*Jesus said: 'Blessed are the meek, for they shall inherit the earth'
(Matt. 5.5) and described himself as 'meek and lowly in heart'
(Matt. 11:29).*

*Pray for those who are lifting up their heads and hearing the calling to
join in God's mission to transform the earth; that they may find new
dignity in that calling, even though they are beset by inbred fears of the
powerful. Let God's indwelling Spirit enable them to come to their full
stature as those who are destined to turn the world upside down, as did
the one who was 'meek and lowly in heart'.*

Not only is Church language very unrepresentative of the languages of humanity, the rhythms of Church activities may bear little relationship to the natural rhythms of thought and action in the world. An experience from our twelve years service in the parish of Rosyth illustrates this.

About twenty people from the congregation met to discuss whether we should start an industrial group. They talked it through. 'Yes,' they concluded, 'provided there is no Bible study as part of the package.' I protested. They would not budge. The industrial group was founded on their terms.

About a year later, they said, 'We need the Bible.' 'I told you that a year ago!' I replied. As to a little child, they explained, 'A year ago we did not need it. We had to learn to look at the dockyard with new eyes. It's now that we have learned what to focus on that we need the Bible, not a year ago.' From then on we wrestled with the Bible for light on the situations they faced.

About two years later, the group stopped meeting. I could get no explanation from the members. A year later they came back wanting to restart. 'But why did you give it up in the first place?' I asked.

Patiently, again as to a little child, they explained. 'Once we were clear about what our faith demanded it was in the Dockyard we had to work things through, so there wasn't much point meeting on Church premises.'

'In that case,' I asked, 'why are you back wanting to start the group again?' 'There are fresh developments. We need the industrial group again to get straight on how we handle the next lot of challenges.'

* * *

REFLECTION

Sister Helen, a Sri Lankan woman working in Belgium, spoke to us about the 'Fourth World' Christian community to which she belonged. Most members did heavy manual work though two or three were professionals. It was their practice to take something which deeply affected them in their ordinary life, find some written comment which illuminated this, consult the Bible and then think about the meaning of the issue in terms of their ordinary, daily actions.

The last two meetings she attended focused on eating. An article one of them had read compared the attitude of a factory owner and a worker to food. The proprietor was indifferent, only wanted to eat when it suited him and did not appreciate even the very excellent food provided for him. The worker was deeply appreciative of his food. He felt he had worked for it, and in some sense had produced it. He saw it as life-giving to him and his family. It was something sacred, near to the heart of life. He realized that we eat because we love life and because we love to have our dear ones continuing to live vitally.

A theme such as this led into much broader areas of social concern. For instance, her group had already gone on to ask about a hunger strike in a prison nearby. What was it that made people willing to give up that life-giving thing, food, until they had achieved some end? There had to be some serious affront to their humanity to bring them to such a pass. The group decided to look further into this and see where any fight for justice should involve them as well.

The ordinary rhythms of life can thus lead to fresh wonder and delight at God's manifold provision for the created order. Deep theological insights emerge to enrich perceptions of how God is at work in daily life.

PRAYER

Ask God's forgiveness if you have imposed the rhythm of life which suits you, on others – in the family, in the Church, at work, at leisure;

– and offer the amendment of life which comes from learning to appreciate different ways and styles of doing things.

ESTABLISHING NEW COMMUNITY

In Barquisimeto, Venezuela, there was a great gulf between Roman Catholics and Protestants in general and between the Pentecostal and RC communities in particular. Before my journey there, I had been alerted to that fact and had discovered that, in the city itself, there was a Roman Catholic charismatic community. I took the opportunity to invite two of the community members, one a priest and one a lay person, to share in our discussions held at a Pentecostal centre.

In return, the Roman Catholics invited us to hold one of our meetings on their Church premises. Some quiet negotiation resulted in this being timed for when there would be a charismatic service in the church itself. When we arrived, the service had already started. In a circle around the priest, a small company were gathered in what was quite a large church. I invited the leader of the Pentecostal community to take five minutes or so just to find what was happening in the church and then come to the meeting with us. Ten or fifteen minutes later he had not appeared. I went to check, and found he had moved from the back of the church towards the charismatic group. He was standing behind a pillar, listening and watching intently. We got on with the meeting without him. After about half an hour, I slipped out again. He had joined the company, and was participating in the worship enthusiastically.

The service and our meeting finished about the same time. I met a man who could hardly get over this momentous experience. That night he spoke to his fellow Pentecostals. 'They pray and preach as we do,' he said. 'They worship as we do. They speak in tongues as we do. They are subject to the Spirit as we are. In spite of all that we have experienced at their hands in the past, we must now think of these Roman Catholics no longer as enemies but as brothers and sisters in the faith.'

* * *

'There is one body and one Spirit just as also you were called in one hope of your calling; one Lord, one faith, one baptism; one God and Father of all who is over all and through all and in all.' (Ephesians 4.4-6)

PRAYER

Father, Son and Holy Spirit, in you we live and move and have our being. It is not just to the Church but to the whole world that you are the source of life. In your life we find life – the true way for the world.

We give thanks for those who throughout history have persisted in their search for truth as did the Wise Men from the East, following the light they saw and looking for more light;

– asking forgiveness for ways in which we shut ourselves off from unfamiliar truth, we pray that the community of faith may be open to whatever you will teach, from whatever quarter.

We give thanks for those called heretics who explore the frontiers of belief, unprepared to accept aspects of faith which to them are not credible;

– asking forgiveness for ways in which we shut ourselves off from unfamiliar company, we pray for the openness of the community of faith to those who do not follow orthodox paths.

We give thanks for Christians who, having known persecution at the hands of other Christians, remain open to transformed relationships;

– asking forgiveness for our own entrenchment in set positions. We pray that members of different denominations, without betraying their traditions, may get alongside one another ready to discard old fears.

We give thanks for ecumenical bodies which pave the way for new relationships between Churches;

– asking forgiveness for any slackness on our part in knitting up the broken fabric of these relationships, we pray that Christians may discover one another's true face in engagement for the establishment of justice, truth and peace in your world

  that the Church may seek only that unity

  which is founded on the Trinity

  and is for the healing and blessing of the whole Creation

Amen.

At Selly Oak Colleges, a tutor at Fircroft Industrial College was asked why none of the Fircroft students took part in the weekly service of worship. He seemed relieved to have such an easy question to answer. 'They had Religious Education at school,' he replied. In his experience students had instinctively placed items in their school curricula in two categories: what smacked of a middle-class culture and could be kicked behind them when they left, and what had a genuine place within their own culture. Unwittingly RE teachers had drawn upon values, assumptions and examples which the pupils recognized as belonging to an alien middle-class world. Worship was part of that world. It was not for them.

Apprentices were sent by their training officers to Scottish Churches House to broaden their horizons. There, time and place for the Bible had to be sensitively calculated. It had to be an integral part of their thinking and not brought in artificially. One morning we were dealing with strikes. The apprentices got deep into the question of how natural resources and the power entrusted to human beings were to be constructively developed. At one point I whipped out Bibles, directed attention to early parts of Genesis, asked if they found good insights there, listened to their responses and five minutes later had the Bibles back on the shelves.

The apprentices went off to lunch and I went off to attend to some other matter. On my return to the room where we had met, a few minutes later, I surprised a young man who had stayed behind. He was circling the room with his hands clasped high above his head in triumph as if his team had just won the cup. He was startled at my appearance but explained, 'When I was a young lad, the Bible meant a lot to me. When I got into my teens, I thought I had to choose between the real world of industry and that fairy-tale world. So I dumped the Bible. Today I found that I don't need to choose one or the other. They belong. The Bible is about living in the real world.'

* * *

'... there is no distinction between Greek and Jew, circumcised and uncircumcised, barbarian, Scythian, slave and freeborn, but Christ is all and in all.' (Colossians 3.11)

REFLECTION

In renewed humanity is there to be no distinction between upper, middle and working classes?

There are those who are class defined but not class-bound:

Cunninghame Graham would lunch off silver, and then go and speak in Glasgow Green in the pouring rain, urging the disadvantaged to fight for their rights. He gave himself to that struggle while remaining an aristocrat.

People can, as Jesus did, choose downward mobility. But they can still be marked by class assumptions. It is promised that in Jesus Christ we can step free of these, through his indwelling power.

Is the Church class-bound, seeking to assimilate others to a limited way of looking at life, of valuing it? If so, is it learning to step free?

At one stage of its life the French (McAll) Industrial Mission found a number of proletarians attracted by the gospel and eventually eager to join the Christian community, So they introduced them to the local Church. That finished it. The Christian faith was clearly not for the likes of them. They felt they had to fit in or give up. They gave up. Others still came forward. The Mission changed course. It kept these new converts together in one company over the years, examining the Christian faith from a proletarian perspective and developing worship which belonged to their own culture. Only after six or seven years was the group introduced to the local Church. Then the sparks flew! It was not, this time, a question of newcomers either being assimilated to an alien class background or getting out. There was mutual challenge, mutual learning and rough but fruitful encounters.

Is the Church you know class-bound? Is the gospel class-bound? If the Church is, examine ways of helping it to break out of bondage, starting from where you are.

The parish church of Rosyth was in a situation of breakdown when Margaret and I arrived in 1948. I saw that the role of the kirk session could prove formative in building up the congregation. Early on, I suggested that we start meetings with Bible study.

The response was anything but enthusiastic: 'We might look at that one bonny day – next business!' However, I persisted. At last, grudgingly, it was agreed that we open with quarter of an hour of Bible study. Then half of the session turned up with apologies a quarter of an hour late. Bible study with the others was like drawing blood out of a stone.

Frustration itself can be productive. At one point a painter from the Dockyard rose and said, 'I'm fed up with this. It's neither one thing nor the other. I move that, for a year, we do half-an-hour's Bible study, and that we all turn up and take part. If it hasn't worked when the year is up, we kill it stone dead.'

It was unanimously agreed. Elders became fascinated by the relevance of biblical texts to their daily life. They participated eagerly and did not notice when the year had passed. After about eighteen months the painter rose again: 'At first I got this all wrong. Earlier when I mentioned the possibility of Bible study to my wife she said, "It's 11 o'clock before you're home as it is. With bible study it will be midnight." It hasn't been like that. Bible study affects the whole Session agenda. Things we would once have spent half-an-hour on we now get rid of in half-a-minute. We have learned to concentrate on essentials. I move that, from now on, we have an hour's Bible study to start each meeting.' This was unanimously agreed. From that time on, the only problem was stopping them after the hour.

They became a biblically-equipped avant garde, leading the congregation beyond their existing perspectives and ideas. So many young people pressed in that we had to establish four Bible classes to cope with them. An elder was made responsible for each. When I was elsewhere on a Sunday, the elders conducted the morning and evening services.

* * *

I have not called you servants, for the servant does not know what his master is doing; but I have called your friends, for all that I have heard from my Father I have made known to you.' (John 15.15)

PRAYER

Lord Christ

Through you all worlds were made; in you all human beings are known with their pretences stripped away; yet you created beings who are to be partakers of the uncreated light. You humble us, making us party to your purpose of love. You shame us, trusting us and taking us into your confidence. You bless us, giving us access to the thoughts of the most High through whom we may have life. This happens through your grace, undeserved. Bless the Lord, O my soul, and all that is within me, bless God's holy name.

We give thanks for those of old time, who struggled to understand the divine judging and healing presence in human life, and left us testimonies which have helped us to discern more clearly your nature and mission.

We give thanks for those who have struggled with words to convey to others the mighty acts and their meaning; for those who wove them into powerful stories given by word of mouth and those who recorded them in writings, drama, poetry and dance, providing for us a heritage of enlightenment.

We give thanks for scholars who worked with integrity to open up the scriptures that we might discern more clearly their meaning and message; and for all sorts of uneducated folk who bring them alive by living out their message.

We give thanks for one another as we challenge and enlighten one another in the struggle for light which the Holy Spirit makes fruitful.

Lord Christ, who on an Emmaus journey opened the Scriptures so that disciples might read them with fresh eyes, journey with us, we pray

– that we may see ever more clearly your will for human life;

– that we may respond to your invitation to share in transforming it;

– that the trust you repose in us by granting us life may be met with an answering, imaginative obedience;

– that you may not have suffered in vain, nor we lived in vain.

We ask it for your own name's sake

Amen.

Margaret combined grace with toughness. Faced with a practical problem, she would take time to get the measure of it, then roll up her sleeves and tackle it with intelligence and energy.

When we moved to the parish of Rosyth in 1948, it soon became clear that we needed a car to tackle the job. A friend in Edinburgh had one for sale, a 23 year old Baby Austin. One problem was the then prohibitive cost of £80. But my parents realized that the care of parish of 14,000 people required mechanical assistance. They provided £50 and we raised the rest.

The other problem was the car itself. I don't think Margaret would have agreed to buy it had she seen it before it drew up at our gate. The body was good, the engine was good but the inside was like a decrepit hen-house. She came down the path, took stock, said not a word. A few hours later she remarked, 'I could dye that mill felt green.' I was the signal I was waiting for. We could get going on the renovation.

The whole interior, except for the bucket seats, was stripped out. I made plywood panels for the sides covering them with furniture plastic, and cut down a chair to make a new back seat. Margaret made covers for all the seats. The car looked new. The people of Rosyth christened it 'the wee green pea'. Whenever it appeared they would stop and wave. It became a character in its own right.

It provided a parable of life. When I was given expenses to cover my costs when I was taking part in some conference or other on the Continent, it offered opportunity to take a few days holiday once the conference was over. We loaded the camping equipment onto a roof rack which I had made out of half a playpen, and took off. I had to cultivate a split mind. One half of me enjoyed the holiday. The other half was not content until everyone was safely home. That's how it is with life. The present is here to be relished. But it is only when life is completed and handed back to the Maker that we can be at peace, finally.

* * *

PRAYER

Lord God, Lord of all life,

You sustain the world and carry it forward from day to day, providing firm earth to walk on, life-giving air to breathe, food to give energy and add savour, companions for the road. Your rain and sun fall on the just and unjust alike. You are the great upholder. For all our squandering of your gifts, you continue to supply our needs.

We give thanks for those who stand with you in this task: for those who cook food in homes and restaurants; for those who make and repair cars which will be safe on the roads; for those who construct the roads, and those who drive trucks over them to distribute supplies; for those who depend on rail or bus travel to allow them to fulfil tasks; for those who create national and regional policies which help life to be carried forward effectively and compassionately.

We confess failure to appreciate the strain involved in working on conveyor belts, while recognizing the boon of reliable machines. We confess our lack of involvement in the battles for justice to be established on the shop floor.

We confess negligence in caring for this planet you have provided both for us and for our children's children.

Forgive us, we pray. Help us to amend our lives.

Teach us to use the products made by other minds and hands appreciating the thought and energy invested in their production.

Teach us to cherish all the life of this planet, that future generations may bless us.

May we take each day as a gift to relish; and still be concerned that we may hear your verdict 'Well done!' when we hand back our lives to you at the end.

All through your grace
Amen.

PRAYER AVAILS

VISITING ED DE LA TORRE IN JAIL, 1977

Mommy de la Torre seemed to live constantly in prayer. As she went about her daily work and life it was as if she were picking up signals all the time about how to manage the way ahead.

We went by bus to the prison camp. At that time visiting was restricted. I had no permit to get in. She seemed to be looking for directions about what to do. Finally her brow cleared. 'We are to play this straight.' We went to the reception room at the jail without more ado.

Whenever the commandant set eyes on Mommy he concentrated all his attention on her. She reared pigs. He wanted one of the piglets as a free gift. He was so intent on this that when she said, 'I have this other friend with me,' he waived me aside to a table where passes were provided, without shifting his attention from Mommy. My credentials were not asked for. There was no examination. I was given the pass. Whether it was agreed that he should get his piglet or not, we got through safely to the next stage. The blindness of greed was our ally.

In the inner court of the prison, there was a guard. He looked at my pass and then said to me, 'What are you doing with that tape recorder?' 'I want to get the thoughts of my friend Ed in his own words,' I said. 'You will get no further unless you leave that here,' said the guard. So I left my tape recorder, to be collected on my way back. The man looked as if he had been on a long shift and was very tired. The taking of the tape recorder was proof to his superiors that he was alert. The genuineness of my credentials did not bother him. It seemed to me that I was encountering another kind of blindness.

In much the same way that Peter walked out of jail (Act 12.1-17), we walked in. In each case prayer opened gates.

* * *

Prayer is waiting, open to the will of God
rapt, attentive, eager for God's voice,
laying cares and pressing worries at God's feet
learning in God's presence to rejoice.
    We're folk of the Way
    who watch and pray
    while still it's day

Prayer is sighing, deep within our restless hearts
forming sounds which words cannot express,
while the Spirit, to the joy of God the Lord
hears, interprets, succours our distress.
    We're folk ...

Prayer is working, flexing muscles of the mind,
bodies offered as a sacrifice,
spirits active – building what will stand secure
and outlast the rule of fear and lies.
    We're folk ...

Prayer's harassment, giving God and man no peace
till they vindicate the poor and weak
where exploited cry in want and misery
there constrained to ask and knock and seek.
    We're folk ...

Prayer's reflection, meditating on God's Word
and the world Christ came to make God's own
till that strong Word penetrates our kingdoms here
and transforms them to be God's alone.
    We're folk ...

WORSHIP RENEWS LIFE

A SERVICE IN AN INDIAN VILLAGE, GUATEMALA

The church was packed. Men and women occupied separate sides. It was the women who did most of the singing. That day, for the first time ever, two women also read from the Old Testament and the Epistle. The priest had the custom of wearing informal clothes up to the point where the service was ready to start, then of putting on a cassock and stole (of local embroidery) in front of the people, removing them immediately the service ended. It made clear that the special dress did not denote membership of a different caste; rather that the worship was led by a specially appointed representative, whose function began and ended with the service.

In front of the church on the right was a black Christ on his cross, balanced on the other side, by a white Virgin Mary. There were flowers, there were saints and symbols, and, in the centre, a kind of box-tent for the reserved sacrament. The reading was on the Good Samaritan.

The sermon was a dialogue with the people. At one point they were asked if they felt assaulted as was the Jew in the story. 'Yes,' they said. 'By what?' asked the priest. 'By illness,' one said. The main attack on the life of the community, they said, came by way of the river. The village was built on both sides of an almost-dry gorge which had been adopted by the city of Guatemala, without consultation with the people, as a sewage outlet.

The people saw the gospel as an invitation to get to grips with this situation and to fight to change it. Mention was made of the latest priest to be killed and the people calmly faced up to the realization that they were called to live as God's children, transforming life, even if that meant the risk of death.

The prayers which followed came from the congregation, a good number of men and women participating. The peace was given, hand on one another's shoulders. All the adults received the communion.

* * *

'The foolishness of God is wiser than men and the weakness of God is stronger than men. Consider your calling, friends: there are not many wise according to human standards, not many mighty, not many noble: but God has chosen the foolish things of the world to shame the wise, and God has chosen the weak things of the world to shame the things which are strong.'
(1 Corinthians 1.25-27)

'When you assemble each one participates contributing a song, a lesson, a revelation, a tongue, an interpretation.'
(1 Corinthians 14.26)

REFLECTION

Consider the power released into the world when poor people seek the face of God and learn to trust in God:
– among whom the gifts of the Spirit are distributed so that all have a contribution to make in building up worship;
– who, insignificant on the world's reckoning, are those who stand with God holding the universe on a true course;
– who are the butt of the powerful who use their space as a rubbish tip;
– before whom principalities and powers should tremble did they but appreciate God's way of changing history, and of dealing with those who treat harshly the 'little ones who look to me'.

By worship the world is held up to God to be cleansed and made wholesome:
– by worship, ordinary folk are affirmed in the presence of the Most High;
– by worship the gifted nature of the whole community is made evident;
– by worship the gates of hell are assaulted.

PRAYER

Pray that
– the gift of worship may be so appreciated as to become fundamentally renewed wherever it grows stale;
– the endowments of the Spirit, distributed among all, may not be quenched but released so that worship becomes rich and dynamic;
– rooting in God may lead to fruiting in the world.
Ask this in the name of him who is the Way, the Truth, the Life
Amen.

GIVING AND RECEIVING

ROGER DESIR, HAITI, 1972

Q. Tell me about the Church services here.

A. I rode on horseback out into the mountains of Leogan. When I walked into the church for the Harvest Festival service I was really thrilled to see there were two banana trees tied to the poles by the communion rail, and, on and around the altar, there were a lot of mangoes, oranges, grapefruit, bananas, rice, beans, peanuts and so on. Really, it was thrilling for me to see these poor people's generosity.

Q. You said this suggested to you points about the way we should give aid to developing countries?

A. We here do not have the huge amount of money that you can tap into in the economic circles of the western world. Yet we do have basic ways of earning money. Look at these people, how sacrificially they respond at harvest time. This is exactly where foreign aid needs to be plugged in. We must not let aid kill the idea of giving on the part of the people. It should be that the more they develop what they have, the more they will give to help the work of the Church.

Ordinarily in the capital Port au Prince, once the people begin to have some kind of income their attitude becomes, 'The Church has money coming from the United States or from elsewhere abroad,' and they stop giving. In the capital you find two groups who have got the wrong end of the stick – a group of poor people who come to the Church because they want to receive something, and people who come but don't give a cent. Contrast that with the countryside and the experience I had the other day. At Leogan I found that there was something genuine – something genuinely Christian – that should be preserved, something basically Haitian.

Aid from abroad is certainly welcome provided that it doesn't kill this spirit of giving among poor people. It should rather be a kind of encouragement for them to feel that in this fellowship and love that we have in Christ, it is better for all of us to give than to receive.

* * *

'Come, let us worship and bow down;

let us kneel before the Lord our Maker;

for he is our God

and we are the people of his pasture

and the sheep of his hand.' (Ps. 95.1-7)

REFLECTION

What privilege it is to be able to approach God in prayer, to worship God with others!

In many traditions, God or the gods have been thought of as self-sufficient, without any need of what creatures can offer. But God the Lord, the Father of our Lord Jesus Christ delights in our approach, cherishes our praise, receives with gladness the tribute of our lives.

Through prayer and worship we are helped to get life straight, in true proportion. When we stand in awe before God's great giving, the springs of generous response in us can be touched. It becomes a joy to offer ourselves, all that we have, all that we are. In prayer and worship we can put the whole fabric of created life willingly back in God's hands where it belongs, to its healing.

Through prayer and worship we can come level with ourselves, and at this or that point stop living a lie. We can share in the brokenness of the world and bring its sins to God, that the whole of nature and social and political life may be transformed through forgiveness.

What a grace it is that we can speak with the most High God in solitude.

What a grace it is to be able to pray with others, their insight and concern enlarging our own.

What a grace it is to go in a great company to join that great company beyond death who live delighting in God; and with them raise hearts and voices in psalms and hymns of praise to the Most High.

To whom be glory for ever
Amen.

PEOPLE'S WORSHIP

A section of the congregation, in particular those who were to the fore in basic Christian communities, had gone to the 'Via Crucis' procession led by a priest, Father D'Escoto. It was a testimony to fellow Nicaraguans and to the world that what the people had set their hearts on was peace, even though they knew that this could mean suffering, taking the Way of the Cross.

Archbishop Ovando y Bravo had not acknowledged the procession and had told his bishops to ignore it. But, on the days in which I was in Managua, the bishop of the area which the procession traversed had met and welcomed it and had presented a Bible as a sign of the significance of constant obedience to the Word of God.

In Nicaragua you find many new hymns whose themes have been deeply influenced by the revolution. They were gifts received in the journey of faith. Where there was rejoicing in new freedom and hope, there was also a keen awareness of the cost of winning and maintaining such freedom. The hymns were sung with great pain.

The life of the congregation draws vitality from seven basic Christian communities. During the week they had met, worshipped, studied the relevant biblical texts, shared insights for living, and shared concerns for prayer. All this was drawn into the parish worship. From that worship there was a reverse flow to strengthen and nourish the small communities.

That Sunday the sermon was on the Transfiguration of Christ, and the union of suffering and triumph which that portended. The priest merely started it off. He then asked members of the congregation to build it up and four or five people took hold of the microphone and contributed. When it was time for intercessions it was again the members of the congregation who identified items for prayer or who led the prayer. When it came to the mass, those present took the host, dipped it in the wine and partook. You could almost hear Christ saying, 'This is my body!' meaning the whole Church worshipping, preaching, praying, partaking.

* * *

*'You are a chosen race, a royal priesthood, a holy nation, a
people for God's own possession, that you may proclaim the
excellencies of him who has called you out of darkness into his
marvellous light: for you were once not a people but now you
are the people of God.' (1 Peter 2.9-10)*

PRAYER

*Holy Spirit of God, you have raised up your people to exercise priesthood
with Jesus Christ the High Priest and distributed gifts among the
members that they might play their part in his work. We bless you for
what our eyes see in our time. We praise you for those whom you have
touched to life who were once treated as of little worth. We rejoice that,
all over the world, your spirit inspires slaves and slave girls to prophesy, old men to dream dreams and young men to see visions; so that a
new world awaits, to the eye of faith.*

*We bless you for Church leaders, who, as with priests in the early Church
have been prepared to make community with a new Church 'born from
below', laying aside the security of protected status.*

*We bless you that what you had joined and human beings put asunder are
united once again; that the praying people are the politically involved,
evangelicals are ecumenical, money and mysticism belong together on
the way of obedience.*

*We bless you for methods of mutual nourishment and instruction which
help the priestly people to grow to the measure of the stature of the
fullness of Christ.*

*We bless you for theology recovered as the people's work and the people's
resource; and that the work of scholars finds new relevance and
fruitfulness when located at the heart of believing communities.*

This is the Lord's doing and it is marvellous in our eyes.

*Accept the praise and thanksgiving which we offer in Jesus Christ's name
Amen.*

In Rosyth Parish Church, in the late 1940s and throughout the 1950s, Bible study became the basis for a whole range of activities.

The biggest risk and the biggest reward was when the whole congregation was given the sermon to preach. For this to happen, there had to be a public concern which everyone felt keenly about – such as a threat to close the Dockyard, or an outbreak of juvenile delinquency, or sewage carried into a school by bad drainage while different authorities passed the buck. Whatever the issue, it raised deep questions about what life is for.

Relevant passages of Scripture were given out about ten days beforehand. Throughout the community small groups formed and neighbours were approached: 'You've got to help us think through what light the Bible throws on such-and-such a situation.' 'But I'm a Roman Catholic!' – 'We need Roman Catholics.' 'But I'm an atheist!' – 'Good. We're short of atheists.'

On the Sunday in question 130 to 140 folk would gather. After the first part of the worship, I would go to the centre of the communion table with two people on each side. Their job was to offer one sentence each, drawing from scripture what they thought might illuminate the situation facing the community. Then it was up to the congregation.

Unfailingly surprised at themselves, they rose to the occasion and built up the sermon from that point, maybe thirty or so contributing. There was no need to intervene except to draw the communal sermon to a close and round off the proceedings with worship.

The discipline was quite remarkable. If one speaker went off on a tangent, the succeeding one would bring the others back on course. A congregational mind seemed to come into being to guide the development of the communal sermon.

The effect was rich beyond words, as people drew upon a great variety of experiences of life and related these to their wrestling with the scriptures.

* * *

'Behold a great multitude which no one could number, from every nation and people and tongue, standing before the throne and before the Lamb, clothed in white robes with palm branches in their hands, cry out with a loud voice saying "Salvation to our God who sits on the throne and to the Lamb."'
(Rev. 7.9-10)

PRAYER

Lord God, I give you thanks that those I have rubbed shoulders with daily in the street, at work, at home, at play, now departed this life, are in a great company, whose lives are made complete before you, and that they are still at one with us.

I give thanks that the saints on earth are not spiritual athletes but all kinds of ordinary folk whom you have loved to life:

– that people who are reluctant to try new ways may, with persistence, make discoveries which give life to a whole community;

– that deep in ordinary folk are all the resources you need to renew the whole Creation, and that we are called, in union with the Holy Spirit, to release them in one another.

Lord God, as we go about our lives, give us new eyes, that we may see Jesus Christ in the folk around, and believe that the Spirit affirms them in ways we may not at first perceive, and calls them to be your people. With these new eyes, enable us to discern, in the daily routines in which folk engage, your hand transforming the world; and through their gifts, the world being lifted up to you for healing and blessing.

We pray for ourselves, asking for the grace of hearing ears and understanding hearts. Make us responsive to the Spirit in this life that at the end, we may join that great throng, your rag-tag-and-bobtail army of unlikely people, who see you face to face and rejoice with joy unspeakable in your eternal presence,

and to you be the glory for ever
Amen.

In the 1960s, Scottish Churches House became established as a common base for Churches in Scotland. The activities which were to characterize the House were carefully thought out. Among other options, we looked at the retreat tradition, and concluded that it was all washed up – a monastic exercise, adapted for clergy then adjusted for laity, remote from its own origins, not meeting people where they were. We also concluded that the no-retreat tradition was all washed up. People needed space and quiet and time to take stock of life. So we went on a search to find new ways forward.

An industrial chaplain helped us. He told us of a trade-union convener who chaired his committee through its agenda and ended in some such way as this: 'We've talked things out, we've made decisions. But each of us needs to think through the way in which we put decisions into practice right where we are. We'll have five minutes quiet to work on that.' At the end he put on his cap and said, 'Well, that's it!' which was a sort of benediction.

Encouraged by this sign of people's natural recourse to silence, we tried several approaches. One was tripartite. In each session there would be a lead for thinking; then there would be a ruminating period; then a period of silence for appropriation. The ruminating period was one in which people stayed together and could either remain silent or call on the resources of others or share new perceptions.

New constituencies became aware of our 'discovery' approach. On one occasion four miners signed on. After two sessions one of them came to me, for all the world like a shop steward – awkward but determined to make a point: 'This silence thing is killin' us. We just become blank. We canna mak' anything out o' that kind of caper.'

We sat down, talked it through, decided to try what I dubbed a 'streaky bacon' approach – three minutes input, three minutes rumination, three minutes silence repeated through a session. It sounds odd, but it worked for that particular company. Before the last two sessions the miner's representative asked to see me again: 'We're wondering whether we could have a slab of silence in each o' the last two sessions. We think we could use it now.'

* * *

PRAYER

Pray for those who need space:

– young people wanting to shape out a life of their own, feeling constricted by parental oversight while often quietly appreciating the disciplined framework parents provide; parents constricted by the constant demands young people make on time and energy, leaving little room for their own life;

– young people sleeping in cardboard boxes, their hours filled with the search for enough to eat; or leaving home having suffered abuse to seek opportunity to make something of life – so often becoming a prey to drugs and prostitution, yet also claiming an inheritance of freedom;

– families mewed up in bed-and-breakfast accommodation, living on top of one another, scarcely able to breathe their own air, with children crying through the night, nerves constantly on edge;

– people dominated by others, unfree to grow as themselves;

– those caught in systems, who are judged according to their ability to keep the systems going, not treated as having worth in themselves;

– those whose ill-health takes up all their fighting energies.

Reflect on Jesus' saying, 'I am come that they might have life and have it more abundantly,' in light of the above.

SELF-EXAMINATION

Do I give people around me the space they need?

Do I allow myself the space I need?

How am I fighting systems which deny folk space for growth?

Where am I engaged in fighting for development space for poorer, debt-ridden nations?

It is part of the discipline of members of the Iona Community that we plan each day recognizing that the time afforded to us is a gift and that we are accountable to God for its use. This does not mean that we commit ourselves to cramming it with religious duties and good works. We are also to honour our families by making time for them. We are to honour our own lives, find space to be ourselves. We are to work out some wise balance of the energy we spend in Church-based and world-based involvements. We are to take enough rest, and care responsibly for our families and health.

The weight of parish work in Rosyth was so heavy that holidays afforded an immense relief. On one occasion, Margaret, myself and our children went to Rothesay for a holiday. Day after day the tiredness continued to engulf me. It seemed that nothing could shift it. Then one day it was as if God spoke to me: 'Who do you think you are?'

'Your faithful servant, I hope.'

'Some faithful servant! What do you do first thing in the morning when you wake?'

'Prayers for the parish.'

'Do you think I can't look after my own shop while you are away and give you the chance of a proper holiday?'

The burden dropped from me. After that holiday I came back refreshed. Not until then had it struck me – we need a break from prayer responsibilities as well as others.

* * *

SELF-EXAMINATION

Am I offering back my whole life to God, each day?

No other life anywhere in the world at any point of human history is the mirror of mine. Do I treasure its uniqueness, insist on space to be myself?

Whatever other people think I should make of my talents and opportunities, am I open to learn the purpose for which God has given me this particular life? At the end of the day, will I have played my part in rooting values of the Kingdom where my life is set?

My vocation is to be fulfilled in a family of parents, brothers and sisters; or of my partner and our children; or of a small community of friends. Do I neglect them, or use them just when it suits me? Do I lay aside time really to appreciate and nourish close, committed relationships? 'Faith, hope, love: these three. But the greatest of them all is love.' (1 Corinthians 13.13) How is my love expressed?

I have not chosen my race or nation. Do I contribute to its life, supportively and critically? Do I make my contribution with an awareness, which I am ready to share with others, that all races and nations were called by God to belong to one community. Have I worked out a true proportioning of Church-based and world-based commitments so that they instruct each other?

Have I learned to say 'no' to requests which could swamp me?

Am I prepared to be available in situations which I don't like facing, in which I could help people to tackle the challenges of life more creatively?

'So teach us to number our days that we may apply our hearts unto wisdom.' (Ps. 90.12)

God the Lord, every part of my life is a trust from you. It is with my whole being that I am called to respond to that trust. Save me from neglecting any of the assignments and relationships which make up my life. Save me from being overwhelmed – my sufficiency is of you and not of myself.

At the end of the day have mercy on my soul; and grant that none of those who have been tied in the bundle of life with me may perish because of any defect on my part.

In Jesus Christ's name
Amen.

Margaret and I arrived at the fishing village of Bagakay in Negros in the Philippines in 1982, with a sister of the Good Shepherd who had offered to act as guide and interpreter. The people of the village numbered about fifty and they gathered to meet with us in one of the larger rooms.

The village seemed a prosperous place. To the right were fish ponds, to the left were harvested fields and grain drying in the sun, and in front was the open sea. But the villagers did not own the fishponds. They did all the work for a pittance while others got the profits. They did not own the land and a large proportion of the crop, produced solely by their efforts, had to go to the landowner. Japanese trawlers were using the latest netting technology to scoop out great quantities of fish and they were destroying the sea beds. The villagers were no longer prepared, as they had been previously, to accept their situation fatalistically.

What produced the change? Until the early 1970s, they had thought of the Church as being for rich people in towns, not for the likes of them. Then one of the younger members of the community was given the chance of education. At school he encountered the Bible. The villagers would gather round when he returned and he would read and explain it. They found that Jesus' world was their world! In it they met oppressive landlords, questions of tenants' rights and responsibilities, the tough business of finding and catching fish, uncertain harvests, the lighting and cleaning of houses, the baking of bread. They got hope as they listened. Then they began to use their own minds, and drew more on their own experience, challenging the interpretations of their instructor. They discovered the dignity God gave them as people made in his likeness. They became awkward people, no longer prepared to fit in tamely with the schemes of the powerful.

The authorities labelled the challenge to their power Communist although the people did not know what Communism was. It was the gospel which had given them fresh life and hope. Pressures on them mounted. An old lady summed up their situation to the nods of all around: 'To tell the truth, we are afraid. But God's Word is more powerful than our fears. We will all have to die some day. We have decided we may as well die for a worthwhile cause.'

* * *

'O the depth of the riches both of the wisdom and knowledge of God! How unsearchable are his judgements and unfathomable his ways! For who has known the mind of the Lord or who has become his counsellor? Or who has first given to him, that it might be paid back to him again? For from him and through him and to him are all things, to whom be glory for ever. Amen'
(Romans 11.32-36)

Jesus said: 'I no longer call you slaves for the slave does not know what his master is up to: but I have called you friends for all things that I have heard from my father I have made known to you.' (John 15.15)

PRAYER

God the Lord

We acknowledge your mind to be far beyond our understanding. We bow before it with awe and humility. Beyond all the best thinking and the most imaginative obedience of humankind is the fullness of that loving purpose which brought us into being, the secret of that grand design which will bring Creation to crowning.

We bless you that things hidden from the wise and intelligent are revealed to the simple.

— Save us from placing confidence in biblical words themselves rather than in Jesus Christ, the Word of life.

— Save us from interpretations which serve our own purposes – who are given the community of faith to enlarge and correct our thinking.

— Save us from dependence except on the Spirit of Truth who will guide us into all truth, taking what is of Christ and disclosing it.

We rejoice that in our own day the Bible has new power:

— that it liberates from many kinds of bondage – physical, psychological, spiritual, personal and public;

— that principalities and powers are unmasked and their fate sealed.

Help us all to receive the gifts of the scriptures with meekness because of our little knowledge and with assurance because the Spirit wrestles with our spirits to help us grow into the mind of Christ. In his name we ask this

Amen.

In the early 1970s, basic Christian communities in Rome met for a one-day conference twice yearly. One meeting I attended had a big Roman Catholic majority yet it was a Baptist pastor and some of his people who provided the biblical leadership. I spoke with the pastor afterwards and asked how this unlikely alliance had come about.

'We, Baptists,' he said, 'give great honour to the Bible. We tend to assume that it contains all that matters. So we would gather round it and dig into it and dig into it. After some time it became clear to us that we were giving no significant testimony, making no impact on the life of the neighbourhood. At that point we noticed Roman Catholic groups which were certainly making an impact. We had just enough courage – in spite of the dismissiveness and, at times, persecution which we had suffered at their hands – to go to them and say, "We think you have found something in the Christian faith which we need too." They gave us a warm welcome: "Join us!" they said, so we did. In no time at all they were saying to us, "You are so clued up on the Bible! We are ignoramuses. This is not one-way traffic, it is two-way!" We shared what each had found in the gospel, developing a dynamic relationship with one another and engaging in life in the world.'

'What difference did it make?'

'The first thing we became aware of was that there were homeless people in our area. They had been there, right under our noses, but we had not noticed them. We then discovered that there was a *problem* of homelessness. People were not made homeless by chance or bad management of their resources but by the way "the system" worked. The root of the matter turned out to be City Council priorities. We Baptists had to learn skills in city politics!

'We became clear that concern for the Kingdom of God requires us to give attention both to the faith and to the situations people face in the world. Some basic communities in Rome became merely biblicized or merely politicized. They soon went out of existence. Those which remain are convinced about the double reference of Christian discipleship. Christians must never retreat into the Bible or retreat into politics.'

* * *

SELF-EXAMINATION

Do I enclose myself in my own world of understanding which provides security, resentful of any attempt to open it out, dismissive of alternative ways of looking at life, secretly afraid that my world cannot stand up to exposure to the real world?

Do I enclose the Bible in that world of understanding, fending off unfamiliar approaches, placing my confidence in the way I have always interpreted it, afraid that I will be led astray if I even listen to other interpretations?

Do I make the Bible an all-sufficient source of life, finding in it my security, refusing to offer obedience in the world and to share with others in setting up signs of the Kingdom there.

– Am I afraid that I may compromise my faith and be compromised – as if Jesus did not take that risk?

Do I fence myself off from others, finding in like-minded people my security, unprepared for the light which may come from strange quarters since Christ, the true light, enlightens all.

– Am I afraid I might be converted to new ways – who, like Peter, need to be converted many times until the end of my days?

Let me place my confidence in this:

– God is my only security – to put my final trust in anyone else or anything else including the Bible is idolatry;

– Jesus Christ is the Truth, not words about him; and the truth is established when it is lived out, not just heard in the ear;

the Holy Spirit will lead us into all truth when we take the risks of faith.

Let me hear this as a word of the Lord for me: 'It was for freedom that Christ set us free.' (Galatians 5.1)

NEW LIGHT

One of the kirk session Bible study hours in Rosyth Parish Church had focused on the epileptic boy whom disciples tried to deal with when Jesus was on the Mount of Transfiguration. At the end of the session, I observed that we had got quite deep with one another reflecting on the material. An elder dissented: 'The Bible says that the evil power which had the lad in its grip did not come out except by prayer and fasting. We have done something about prayer but nothing about fasting.'

I reminded the session that when manuscripts were reproduced, all kind of additions might be slipped in by those who hand-copied them. It would be only too easy for a scribe who was an ascetic to add just two words – 'and fasting'– to the original text. The original might well have referred to prayer only as the means whereby the demon in the young lad could be exorcized.

He listened. He jabbed his finger at the appropriate passage: 'It says "and fasting"!'

I tried a different tack. 'There are ways of expressing a disciplined life of faith which are quite appropriate in one part of the world but need not be so in another part. In many countries such as the one in which Jesus lived, fasting was a traditional expression of penitence or expectation. There is no need for us in a different century and in a different country, to feel that it is a way that we should adopt.'

He listened. He spoke four words: 'It says "and fasting"!'

There was nothing for it but to agree that the Bible study to open the next kirk session meeting would be on fasting. That decision led us to the relevant passage in Isaiah 58. It brought home to us that a religious practice of fasting did nothing if life went on as before. Fasting provided positive and creative space in which to get life straight and to prepare oneself for fights against all kinds of injustice and oppression in struggles for the liberation of all peoples.

* * *

'I hate, I reject your festivals
Nor do I delight in your solemn assemblies ....
Take away from me the noise of your hymns,
I will not listen to the music you make:

But let justice roll down like waters,
righteousness like an ever-flowing stream.'
(Amos 5.21-24)

PRAYER

Let us confess:
– our readiness to participate in religious exercises without engagement in
society wherever God calls for justice to be established;
– our unreadiness to listen to those who dig their heels in, who make us
face issues we would otherwise avoid;
– our unwillingness to recognize that we are to spend our lives for the
world, and that worship sends us so to do.

Lord God, you see into our hearts:
sift us and save us, we pray.

Let us give thanks:
that the Bible is in the hands of the Church
not just the hands of specialists but of humble, perceptive folk;
that new light is breaking forth
to challenge stereotyped interpretations;
that, in previously devalued cultures and histories,
people recognize themselves in its pages and find a word of life.

Let us pray:
– for small companies of people who struggle for light, sharing discover-
ies;
– for those who live in new ways, challenging the status quo at great cost;
– for those who make worship a springboard for the doing of justice and
offer up actions in the world to enrich worship;
– for those who insist on being awkward till queries are dealt with;
– for scholars who find a creative role at the heart of the life of the people.
Let us rejoice at the way in which the formation of the World Council of
Churches and the work of Vatican II have released people to put the
Bible at the centre of their lives, acknowledging its authority to shape
their lifestyles.

BAPTISM

IN BASIC CHRISTIAN COMMUNITIES

In the Emmaus Community near Turin, Matteo was six months old when he was baptized in the parish where he then lived. The priest allowed the community to have the kind of service they wanted. The community itself conducted the service. They felt that having the baptism in that situation enabled local people to relate to the community.

Sarah was baptized at the age of three in the community itself and not in the parish church. About seventy people attended – friends and members of other basic Christian communities. In this case, if they had gone to the parish church, they would have had to follow a form of service which they could not honestly affirm. Her name is not found in the parish register but the community has documented her baptism.

One result has been that people in the community have felt much more involved in her growth in faith. Sarah herself was a lively participant in the service and remembers what it meant to her.

Walloon groups in Belgium prefer to wait until a child is one or two years old before baptism. The preparation of the parents and child is directed towards entrance of the child into a Christian community of several families. The baptism takes place at what is judged to be the appropriate point in the life of the community, and it is not formally related to the parish or to the local Church.

A priest is involved but he acts as an auxiliary to the community's receiving of the child. A deep communal understanding of baptism is developing through this practice.

* * *

PART OF A BAPTISM PRAYER PREPARED BY MEMBERS OF ISOLOTTO, A BASIC CHRISTIAN COMMUNITY IN ITALY

This baby who is being presented to the assembly
is a moment of hope and joy.
We welcome him
into this Christian community
not to determine his choice for him
but rather to educate him towards freedom.
If we succeed in this educational task of liberation
his person will be precious to us,
whatever choices he makes;
we will be able to say that we have not suffocated your Spirit
who has given us this gift of new life.
The gesture of pouring water
expresses our awareness of being tied
to the great biblical events,
to all Christian tradition,
and in particular to the baptism of Jesus in the Jordan.
As John stood before Jesus
we also place ourselves before this baby,
before all babies,
before all those who are considered 'nothings' by the wise and
     powerful,
before those discriminated against,
before the least.
We also affirm that it is we who must be baptized;
it is also we who must pass through the water
which is the sign of purification,
of liberation and of untiring struggle
but finally of victory and resurrection.
In this spirit (name of child) we baptize you
in the name of the Father, the Son and the Holy Spirit.

THE MEANING OF THE EUCHARIST

ED DE LA TORRE, INTERVIEWED IN A 'SAFE HOUSE' IN THE PHILIPPINES
IN 1973, WHEN ON THE RUN FROM THE POLICE.

'One Christmas, a group of about a hundred farmers came up here to demand land from the government. We held a midnight mass. We were reflecting on what that meant and I felt that one of them expressed it well when he said, "The Christian meaning of what we are doing is this, no? At the Eucharist we have only a few hosts, only a little bread, and we break it up and give it to each other. Why is this? It is really an act of the poor. There is not enough, that's why we break it up. If there were enough for all we would all get a whole piece."

'Another farmer's observation is even more profound: "Even if there is not enough, we will not follow the logic of the development economists who say, 'Let's first increase the GNP. Then, if there is not enough, we will make sure that we first feed those who are strong enough to work. Others can take their chance.' No! We won't postpone the sharing. There will not be enough for everyone but no one will have nothing."

'The whole point is not abundance or scarcity but that we share in a real celebration. We are not just going to glorify scarcity for scarcity's sake as more heroic. Even more importantly, we are to share what there is available in the period of poverty. What is most important is our solidarity.

'There was no explicit reference in this to the Last Supper but I think the farmer, in his own way, was articulating a very profound Eucharist, which I personally could not achieve with all my priestly training.'

* * *

REFLECTION

Isolotto was Italy's first basic Christian community. When extruded by force from its Church building, it began its existence by celebrating mass, come rain or shine, in the public square of that suburb of Florence in 1968.

The following is part of a Eucharistic reflection, written in conjunction with the children of the community who prepared the sermon and prayers that Sunday.

Jesus thought very highly of children.
He considered them an essential component
of that world of the 'least' and 'the little ones'
upon which society, history and the Kingdom of God rest.
He made himself little
and fully subjected himself to poverty
and partook of the destiny of the masses at the bottom of society.
He was unable to give more of himself than his own life.
He had no money, nor prestige nor influence on the institutions.
This being so, the evening before he died,
after having washed the feet of his disciples,
he took the bread, broke it
and gave it to them saying:
'Take and eat of it, this is my body.'
Then he took a cup, gave thanks
and gave it to them saying:
'This is my blood which is shed for all people.'
We are eating this bread
in communion with Christ
and with all the children and the 'little ones' of the earth.
May God's spirit render this communion effective
so that the invitation of Jesus
to call him father
and one another brothers and sisters
are not vain words.
Amen.

Margaret and I took part in a Eucharistic celebration. Children and adults from flats around gathered together in the priest's flat. Candles were lit to the great delight of the children in particular. There was a small table with a cup and bread and a cross on it.

To start with, there was music and hymns and songs of a contemporary religious character. We then had a Bible reading, the story of the widow who kept harassing the judge until she got justice. The children in particular, with the priest acting as the unjust judge (no child would accept the role), made a dramatic presentation of this biblical parable.

It was remembered that there was somewhere a Hallowe'en mask of an old lady, and one of the children went and found it to take the part of the widow. Thereupon other children, determined not to be left out, went and got a mask of a dog, and a mask of a Red Indian – so there had to be a dog in the story and a Red Indian amongst Jesus' disciples. The parable was acted out.

It was asked how it might be represented in a contemporary way. It was decided that the question of justice might be illustrated by miming a game of basketball. Accordingly the children mimed a basketball game in which the referee turned a blind eye to fouls ignoring the pleas of those offended against. This gave the children an idea of the essential meaning of the parable, particularly when one of the adults helped them to see that God expected them, in any situation, to keep fighting for justice and pleading for justice for themselves and for others.

There were then prayers of approach to the Eucharist, taken by the children. The priest himself took the short act of consecration. The bread and wine were shared among the adults and three of the children, the older ones remaining while the younger ones had gone off to play. There was the giving of the peace with embraces, kisses or handshakes. Further prayers were made by the children, and some hymns ended the service.

* * *

REFLECTION

We're 'in and out' people, Lord God.

In and out of the door of the house – into the world to work, serve, shop, play; and back through that door to draw breath, to be ourselves, to be with our nearest and dearest, to be at peace.

We are in and out of the Church, drawing into worship the happenings, puzzles, frustrations, joys of each week – holding them up to you that you might receive what we've done and who we've been and clean it up that it might shine to your glory; then out into the week to show we are yours by the way we live.

We are in and out of life: wakening each morning to a new day of promise; until there's a day when we don't awaken and are happed away like sheets in a drawer, once they have served their purpose.

We are glad, Lord Christ, that you were also in and out:
– in home and workshop, an apprentice carpenter, learning then plying your trade; and out in the streets and fields, drinking in life that your teaching might be true to it;
– kept in, on the sidelines, seeing the years roll on, for nearly all your life; then thrown out into your mission with all its risks;
– resting in the family at Bethany, then out on a hill, alone on a cross to accomplish our salvation.

We seek to live in you who promised to live in us:
– we bring to you the life we have tried to live out in the world with honesty and imagination – a jumble of true endeavour and of failure to be our true selves, a mixture of self-forgetfulness and self-seeking, of advancement of your cause and of self-advancement;
– through your forgiveness, sort it all out, we pray, clean up our act. Help us to worship you in spirit and in truth so that, when we go out into the world and into each week, we may live to your glory and praise by grace of your indwelling.

We ask it for your own name's sake
Amen.

Sometimes it takes physical movement to open up new avenues for creative relationships.

Dr Fritz Raaflaub of the Basel Mission in Switzerland spent years seeking some basis for a European conference on mission and training in mission. But he found the various mission institutes too diverse in their traditions, emphases, experience, methods of formation and outreach to bring them to one starting line. Out of our reflections on these unsuccessful attempts came the idea of the Snowball Visitation.

The Department of Mission in Selly Oak took the initiative. Two or three staff members would visit mission training institutes of a different traditions, for a few days each. Their aim would be to absorb and appreciate the intention and approach expressed in each particular operation and to develop an open listening relationship with the staff. Only towards the end would questioning and criticism be in order.

The following year, two or three people from one institute visited would join Selly Oak representatives to visit another. Thus awareness of approaches could grow, relationships could develop, critical appraisal could prove mutually beneficial at a time when the Church's mission called for deep rethinking.

First we went to Hermannsburg in Germany, then to Stavanger in Norway. Among the Selly Oak contingent to Norway was Dr Mary Hall, a Roman Catholic. Her openness and dynamism intrigued and delighted Lutherans especially. They voted to make the RC Mission Societies based in Dublin their next stop. We were warmly and hospitably received. By now the visiting party consisted of many denominations, but quickly experienced great solidarity of spirit.

I realized that two masses would be held during our time in Dublin and asked whether not only participation but partaking would be in order. 'Don't ask questions,' came the cheery reply, 'and nobody will raise any.' 'Not good enough,' I answered, 'Do we belong or do we not?' It was an unexpected response and startled them. They thought for a while and then responded, 'You belong! You are invited!' It was a breakthrough.

* * *

'Now the Lord said to Abram: "Go forth from your country and from your relatives and from your father's house to the land which I will show you."' (Genesis 12.1)

'Jacob said, "Surely the lord is in this place and I knew it not."' (Genesis 28.16)

PRAYER

God the Lord, father and mother of all created life, what a love was yours to send your own Son, the living image of your being, to redeem and restore Creation to the purpose for which it was made. Had we been God, we would not have run the risk. We would have bathed in the security of heaven. So we bless you that you are God, not us; that Jesus Christ moved from your side and lived an exposed and vulnerable life among us; that through the Spirit he gives strength to enable us to break with life's securities and move to where we are wanted, where our lives will find true direction and become a blessing to humankind, as was Abram's.

We give thanks that you open ways before us when you find us ready to get up and go:

– that, in the exodus from Egypt a people knew you as one who travelled with them, facing with them the hazards, rejoicing with them in their overcoming, dealing patiently with their backtracking and complaining;

– that, in the exodus accomplished in Jerusalem, all peoples were made inheritors of a new and living way and that today, through the Holy Spirit, we find Jesus Christ journeying beside us, bearing the brunt of our disheartenment and urging us on.

And so we are part of your mission.

– Help us to recognize and never forget, that the mission is yours, not ours, that it is you, not we, who set the terms and provide the promise.

– Help us to make discoveries which establish us in new community, with gifts put within our grasp which had eluded us.

– Help us to search one another out that we may travel together, correcting one another, encouraging one another.

– Help us to be heralds of a love which reach out to the whole Creation and give it life

that we may be children of our Father in heaven,

not disobedient, but found faithful

Amen.

AN INSTINCTIVE SACRAMENTAL ACT

ROSYTH

He was always present at the evening service, and our conversation revealed him to be a convinced and committed Christian, but he would not become a communicant member of the Church. He came from a part of the Outer Isles where the tradition was to become a full member and receive communion only in old age or at the approach of death.

One day he told me he would have to return to his native heath. He had brought his two daughters with him in order that they might find employment. They had done so.

But he had reckoned without the effect on their minds of the change from a remote country situation to a dockyard area. They had begun to show signs of stress. This had become marked enough for the family to decide that they must go home.

He asked me to visit him on a particular night, close to the time of departure. We spoke a bit, prayed a bit, then he told me to wait while he went 'ben the hoose'.

He reappeared with a linen serviette on his arm, and a full glass of whisky on a small tray. He approached me quietly and solemnly and offered the glass. 'This is for what you and I have been to one another under God during my time here,' he said.

I hope that the most rabid teetotaller would have drunk from that glass. It was a sacrament as surely as any formal communion in church. I thought of the woman with the ointment at Jesus' feet. She, too, had to go beyond words to communicate the depth of her feelings.

* * *

REFLECTION

Reflect on the instinct in human beings to express in symbols which have power through the centuries, their anchorage in the deep things of God.

Reflect on the instinct in human beings to offer some visible sign to express what others mean to them: 'Say it with flowers', or a bottle of wine, or some home-baking or a last crust shared.

Reflect on the instinct in human beings to respond to God the Lord: breaking through the ice of rationalistic and materialistic periods in human society to draw afresh on springs of living water.

Reflect on the way in which, through the centuries, the Church has taken advantage of this instinct, making sacramental practice at times a control device.

Reflect on the following experience in the Netherlands.

In the early 1970s some Roman Catholic basic Christian communities decided to take stock of the essential requirements of the gospel. They looked at the Bible. 'It is the priest's book interpreted to suit his purposes: out of the window with it.' They looked at the mass. 'A rigmarole and an instrument of priestly control: out of the window with it.' 'What does the gospel ask of us? To establish justice on earth! That is what we will be about.'

In not much more than a year they gathered together once again and reviewed their experience: 'We don't know what justice is without the Bible. We're not nourished for the struggles without the sacrament.'

They found through life in the world what had eluded them in the Church. Their rediscovery of the significance of the Bible and the Mass brought joy and conviction as conformist acceptance of the Word and sacrament could never have. It was crucial in their pilgrimage that they kept an eye on the discarded tradition in case there was more in it than they had first thought.

PRAYER

Lord God, make me alert to the instinctive sacramental responses of people that I might recognize and honour them, however awkwardly they fit in with traditional religious life.

Lord God, teach your Church a sacramental life which meets people where they are, brings them to you, and nourishes them in the life of the Kingdom.

We ask it in Jesus Christ's name

Amen.

1980. Four hours before I was due to leave for Guatemala from Mexico City, my host, Rev. Dr Gaxiola Gaxiola was alerted on the phone to the fact that my next contacts had been killed, gone underground or fled the country. There would be nobody to meet me at airports in Guatemala and El Salvador. I decided to press on nonetheless.

I duly arrived in Guatemala Airport and there was no one there. Some nuns were on the lookout for friends arriving off the same plane as myself. Just to establish human contact I asked them, knowing their answer beforehand, whether they had seen the sister who was originally to have met me. They said they had not. Then their friends appeared, and they greeted them excitedly. They moved off, talking volubly, to their car.

What was I to do in this situation? I decided I would simply stay around and look forlorn.

The nun who was driving had to make a sweep around the airport frontage to go to the city. At the last moment she looked across and saw me, changed direction, brought the car alongside, and asked, 'Has the sister not turned up?' I said that this was the case. 'Is there some address in Guatemala City which just might be on our route?' I mentioned the only address I had. 'Oh,' said the nun, 'Iglesia la Merced is not far off the route we will be taking. There is one space left in the car. We can take you there.'

They took me to the church house or presbytery and I realized I might not have found it otherwise because it was tucked away in a back street. As we arrived, a young man was putting away his car. It turned out that he was the one person in the whole of Guatemala whose name I still retained as a possible contact. He took me in, and the house became my base.

He told me that if I had arrived five minutes earlier or five minutes later I would have got no answer. Five minutes earlier, he would not have been there; five minutes later no one at that time of night would have answered the door since they could be shot at from the darkened street.

* * *

REFLECTION

Reflect on the strangeness of God's providence:

– actions and journeys which might have proved fruitless, in the end made productive; obstacles removed, dangers circumvented – for some;

– others getting the worst rub of the green every time, their best efforts and hopes crumbling in their hands, seemingly pursued by a malignant fate.

Does God have favourites? Are God's ways just and true?

Some who are looked on as 'the privileged' are actually losers. Having been 'feather-bedded', they fail to become rounded and complete human beings. Some who are looked on as underprivileged outperform them in human qualities and in life-accomplishments.

So is it true that God can take failure and, if it is offered, make more of it than of success? Can God really do exceeding abundantly above all that we ask or think? If this is so, we can have no reason for discouragement if we do not make the grade according to human standards, or for complacency if we do.

Or is that dodging the issue? Let us stand before the mystery, and let us pray.

God the Lord,

We hold up to you those who have never had a chance from the day they were born; those afflicted by illness or injury or abuse in childhood; those bullied at school or deprived of schooling; those who, as adults, have been treated unfairly by authorities, harassed, or robbed of liberty; those spoken to with condescension and, with a sneer, labelled 'inadequates'; all those who are downtrodden – of whom the world is not worthy.

We hold up to you those who, in spite of the most adverse of circumstances, keep a flame of dignity and creativity alight. May they know that you tend that flame.

We offer ourselves in support of weak and despised things and weak and despised people; that in you, they may outshine the mighty,

and to you be the glory for ever

Amen.

I went to the headquarters of the late Archbishop Romero (martyred for fighting for justice) seeking to establish a useful contact with local basic Christian communities.

At reception they were unable to help me. I came out of the main door, wandered to my left and, seemingly by chance, ran into none other than the Archbishop's personal link with basic Christian communities in that area! Once more, with prayer as my only resource to confront the unknown, the journey was to turn out to be productive.

Later that day, when my new contact had gone to his home some miles outside the city, I visited the radio station, coming back to the Archbishop's headquarters only to find everything locked up for the night, including my rucksack and passport. (Because of the pressure put on the Church following Archbishop Romero's stand against injustice, the different parts of the headquarters seemed to be locked up separately and the keys disposed of so that others in the building did not know where they could be found – a device to thwart police and military intrusion.)

So there I was, without any place to stay in that city, where the death squads roamed every night and left a trail of corpses. If I had stayed out all night, I might not have seen the light of day. If I had gone to a hotel, my want of a passport would have meant that the police would have been called and I would have landed in jail. I had but one lifeline – the phone number of my new contact.

He told me that there was a house in town which the occupants had had to abandon because a neighbour – a retired military man hostile to Archbishop Romero – had been putting severe pressure upon them. I could use that house as a shelter for the night.

I seized the chance with both hands. The next morning a very relieved Ian Fraser was able to retrieve his belongings and documents, rejoicing that he was still alive, and not even behind bars.

* * *

PRAYER

Almighty God, father and mother of us all,

We give thanks that, in our time, we see some signs of a Church more truly one than it has been in many past ages; in which the ordained are not protected as they once were from public vilification and from assassination, nor granted separate status; and that Archbishop Romero, as he prophesied, has genuinely risen again in the life of the people, he who was at one with them in his death.

We give thanks for those who are of a conservative turn of mind, such as was Archbishop Romero, who, in their growth and maturing, live through experiences which challenge previously held positions and attitudes, and lead them to take undreamt of stands against injustice.

We give thanks for those with a radical turn of mind who, in their growth and maturing, open themselves up to a fresh appreciation of those things which conserve past gifts and provide continuity;
– who in different ways, contribute to the Church's dynamic unity.

We give thanks for the spread of basic Christian communities which provide signs of that longed for unity:
– in which women, men and children are given equal and honoured place;
– in which prayer and preaching and political action belong together;
– in which the unity of humankind in justice, truth and peace is sought;
– in which baptism is the action of the whole people and the Eucharist the building up of all who share in Christ's ministry;
so that celebration and bearing one another's burdens and struggles for justice belong together in one enterprise of life.

We give thanks for that unity of life which we ourselves may find when we are no longer 'tossed to and fro by every wind of doctrine'
but accept our vocation and allow life to be integrated around it;
and for that unity of humankind which peeps through the veils of war
and injustice in our times, beckoning towards a greater fulfilment.
Above all, we give thanks that the world is in your hands who know how to handle it in love.

Amen.

A NEAR THING (1)

The nearest I came to getting jailed in the Philippines was in 1977. Ferdinand Marcos had decided on a period of special vigilance. He attempted to seal all exits from the country of information which might be detrimental to his seamy regime. Evidence had been assembled about unjust imprisonments, torture, and salvagings (assassinations) – but the channels for getting them to Justice and Peace organizations in different parts of the world had been blocked. I volunteered to try to get them delivered.

Taking my cue from Edgar Allen Poe's story, 'The Letter', I decided that the safest place for the documents might be the most obvious – in my hand luggage. But at the airport I was picked on for a spot check.

The woman who looked through my bag, instead of examining it just for bombs, hand-grenades and so on, demanded what the packets were. I replied that they were letters from friends which could reach their destinations quicker if I posted them in Britain. She asked what was in them. I replied, 'I do not read my friends' letters.' She answered, 'You are getting no further until I find out what is in these letters!' We stood facing one another across the table, the bag between us.

At that point a group of Japanese tourists came up behind me, some pushing at the back because they were late for their plane. Those at the front swept me bodily past the point of search. I grabbed the bag with the documents before the woman could. She held up her hands in defeat and gave up any further attempt to challenge me.

At the next stage, another obstacle appeared – the screening chamber in which tapes and films could be scrubbed. During that period in the Philippines I had taken thirty-two interviews, including that of Trining Herrera, the leader of the Tondo Community, speaking about the severe torture she had suffered. What a loss these tapes would be!

When we landed, tape after tape proved to be unimpaired. Trining's voice went out on the 'Sunday' programme of the BBC, telling of her torture and giving direct testimony to what she had endured.

* * *

'Do not affront or maltreat the stranger, for you were strangers in the land of Egypt.' (Exodus 22.21)

'Pilate then released Barabbas to them; but Jesus he flogged and handed over to be crucified.' (Matthew 27.26)

'I was in prison and you visited me.' (Matthew 25.36)

PRAYER

Lord God, whose Son had no place to lay his head except a Cross,

we pray
– for those who are victims of human brutality;
– for those who languish in jails with no charge made to justify their imprisonment (here pray for some of those identified by Amnesty International ...);
– for those who have little to eat and poor health care;
– for those who are thrown by torture into a nightmare world.

Draw near to give them courage and hope.

– for those who consign others to torture and death;
– for torturers, brutalized in order that they may, in turn, brutalize;
– for guards, offered no option but to follow prison routines;
– for all who consent to systems of oppression;

– for Mothers of the Disappeared, confronting powers-that-be;
– for husbands, wives, children, fathers, mothers of hostages and other victims;
– for those who, like Pilate's wife, begin to see things differently;
– for dissidents and resisters;
– for refugees, their fate at the mercy of laws designed to keep out rather then provide sanctuary; for those without country or roots; for divided families; for victims of war and famine; for those who have no recognized accreditation.

We give thanks
– for countries which welcome strangers; for agencies which disclose to the world atrocities which would otherwise remain hidden; for a growing sense of international responsibility for victims; for the rising of peoples to eradicate different forms of oppression.

Amen.

A NEAR THING (2)

In 1982, after retirement from Selly Oak Colleges, Margaret and I entered the Philippines when Ferdinand Marcos, the dictator, was in the USA being feted by Ronald Reagan. Extra care was taken to vet all who sought entry to the Philippines. The queue moved very slowly towards the passport check-up desk.

My turn came. The man looked at my passport, frowned and consulted the black book at his side in which all manner of undesirables were registered. I slipped round the opposite side of his desk without his noticing. He had turned to 'F'. There I was in all my glory. By the time he had checked through the record, I had taken my place again at the front of the desk. He gave his attention afresh to my passport. His face cleared. We got through safely.

I did not tell Margaret what I saw till we were back in Britain. In the black book I was Rev. Dr Ian M. Fraser, MA, BD, Ph.D, Dean and Head of the Department of Mission, Selly Oak Colleges, Birmingham. On my passport I was Ian M. Fraser, educationalist, Gargunnock. What connection could there possibly be between these two?

The fact that on the previous visit I had taken out reports of tortures, imprisonments and assassinations and sent them to Justice and Peace organizations in different parts of the world must have become known. I think that the most the authorities would have done would have been to keep tabs on me. But was I glad to slip through the net!

My prayers that night included thanksgiving that, while God did not intervene to prevent the rise of dictatorships, she also did not intervene to insist on their competence in keeping records up to date.

* * *

PRAYER

Hold up to God

– *people who check on documents, who can make it difficult for families to be reunited as well as for illegal entry to take place; their superiors who can interpret regulations rigorously or flexibly; government ministers whose preferred legislation may be inhospitable or generous, tolerant or racially biased;*

– *those who man detention centres, and the detainees; prison guards and prisoners; organizations set up to protect the vulnerable;*

– *soldiers, so often given boring routine duties; at times forced to make quick decisions which mean life or death to others in dangerous situations; sent to tasks they hate; at times going over the top; given little thanks for quiet service;*

– *'internationally acceptable' people, who may place little store on the privilege of having a passport which is universally recognized;*

– *refugees, with inadequate papers or none; who flee poverty or persecution;*

– *separated families, longing to be reunited;*

– *wanderers on the face of the earth who have no homeland;*

– *those who shape international legislation and set up courts of appeal to attempt to ensure that justice is done.*

Lord Christ, once a refugee in Egypt hospitably received, so touch the imagination and hearts of those in whose hands the fate of others lies, that they may be your servants acting justly, loving mercy and walking humbly with you.

Strengthen the hands of those who have difficult judgements to make.

We ask it for your own name's sake
Amen.

In Tarlac, the Philippines, a community of farm workers had suffered disaster after disaster. It started with a plague of rats, which, like locusts, ate right though their crops. Next year, the rats came back and did the same thing. The following year, a virus destroyed the whole crop. The year after that, typhoon and flood ruined everything. 'For forty-five days,' said a mother of nine, 'it rained day and night. I gathered my children and said, "Children, this may be the end of the world." At times all we had was one cup of rice for the whole family.'

In May 1974 they were just beginning to get on their feet again. I asked them whether they had come to feel that God had laid a curse upon them, as catastrophe followed catastrophe. 'We felt that God was punishing us for our sinfulness and carelessness,' said one farm worker. His interpretation was at once challenged by others: 'God does not act like that. God never acts like that. It wasn't a punishment, it was a time of testing. We had to go through a time of testing.'

They had developed a new communal way of living. The few who owned fields decided to offer them to the farm labourers, after the rice harvest, to plant mongo (beans). They now take common responsibility for the productive land. If one is ill or away from home, neighbours step in and see that the land is tended. They are a caring and sharing community and none is left out. Even those who for one reason or another cannot work get their portion.

It was natural for them to have a service of worship to greet me when I arrived. There was a hymn, followed by scripture reading. Then fourteen (out of a total company of forty) rose one after the other and built up an exposition of the scriptural text. When the time for prayer came, as many again took part. Living, worshipping, sharing possessions were all of a piece to them. There was not only a sure touch for essentials, but a vision of wholeness.

* * *

REFLECTION

'NATURAL' DISASTERS

Our new awareness of the environment has taught us to recognize human responsibility in what had previously been ascribed to natural causes. Floods occur because forests which had absorbed the rain are felled. People risk building on the sides of volcanoes or on fault lines, and eruptions and earthquakes destroy homes and lives.

But disaster also comes in ways which are quite beyond human reckoning and control, and in ways which cannot be anticipated. God seems to have made a world which has random elements in it. Some people are robbed of goods, or health or life. Some escape. What sense can we make of it? It may be something which will always be beyond us. What we can rest on is what we are given in the gospel:

– that God stays with us in it all;

– that Jesus Christ accepted our human lot, with all its risks;

– that the Spirit can give us resilience to overcome;

– that when each day brings nothing but desolation till death takes us, we know that God knows what it is like to feel abandoned.

For we have before us Jesus Christ's forsakenness and death on a cross.

God honours us by giving us life in which there is risk and suffering. For God means us to mature in faith and to bear one another's burdens.

PRAYER

Mysterious God

Your ways are often beyond our understanding. We get blessed, we get crushed, and there seems to be no good reason for either. We ask, seek, knock and do not receive, or find, or have doors opened. There is that in you which baffles us. Yet it is with awe that we remember that not only this small world but the whole universe is in your hands. It is with awe that we acknowledge that, for all our ignorance and perplexity, you have made us partners in your redeeming work, and that that work will succeed.

Make us ever discontented with the extent of our knowledge. Inspire us to go on asking, seeking, knocking until this world bears more clearly the stamp of your will.

We ask it in Christ's name

Amen.

Read and appropriate Romans 8.31-39 and Ephesians 6.10-18.

TESTING BY HUMAN OPPRESSION (1)

'We are an international order (Notre Dame) and we have five sisters who work as a team. Three of those sisters met William Ramirez. He is the Minister of Transport right now, but he had been the responsible official in the region where our sisters worked.

'He said to them, "You should really go to the mountains and talk to the people there because they have the Word of God. Then when you hear them, go back to your own land and take that Word with you." That was an impressive speech to hear from such a person. They did go up there. It's true, I think that the voice of God is in the people. The sisters have taken the Word back with them.

'Here, in Nicaragua, that fact is very evident because what's really happening is "a love growth" and that's what the Christian message is all about. Jesus, I think, only gave us the one single criterion, or the one sign: "By this everybody will know know that you are my disciples if you have true love for one another." It's not just any kind of love but true love, love that can rise to facing death without fear.

'Nobody wants to die, and we are afraid. But in my experience so far in these two years, one thing I've learned is that death is a Christian experience. I never had that concept before. Being faced with guns [this refers to the depredations of the Contras] really shakes you, yet it doesn't stop you. So there's got to be something nuns like us learn from living with these people at the base of society that brings about a Christian transformation.'

* * *

REFLECTION

We do well to be wary of death. If 'we die like beasts' (Ps. 49), if there is nothing more to living that what is on the level of ordinary human experience, then all that we and others have attempted and seem to have accomplished goes down the drain. Death then robs life of meaning. Also it leaves the powerful to have their way with the world without being called to account.

Yet those who have learned to face death can have greater quality in their living. They have a confidence beyond the human which invests the human with hope and dignity. Young people in El Salvador, hunted by Death Squads, did not surrender their lives easily. They escaped if they could. But if they were cornered and there was no alternative they would say, 'Now we must continue the fight from the other side.'

There is another side. We would not have full confidence that death is not the end had not Jesus Christ tackled death and overcome it on our behalf. Now we know that what has been well done in life need not be lost, but can be gathered into God's large enterprise; that what has been ill done in life can be covered by a comprehensive forgiveness, and that what we are as human beings can be rounded off and made complete beyond this life.

The fight goes on. One company on each side of death struggles to make the prayer 'Your Kingdom come, your will be done on earth as it is in heaven' effective in time and space. We are not separated off from those who have gone before. We are in one community, heartened and encouraged for that part of the battle which falls to us, helped to endure in adversity.

PRAYER

God the Lord, we believe: help our unbelief.

We cannot see beyond the grave; help us to trust and not be afraid. Bring home to us the mighty work of Jesus Christ in overcoming death, that we may make it our own. We give thanks for those who have so learned of you that death has lost its power over them; who, without seeking death, are ready to treat it as a bridge to heightened living in your presence; who strengthen those of us who are weaker to confront and outface the last enemy.

Keep us in touch with those who have completed life's journey on earth, that we may continually rejoice in one another and glorify you who have the last word over every destroyer and despoiler.

In Jesus Christ's name

Amen.

Mrs Trining Herrera, President of the Tondo community of shanty-town dwellers on the foreshore of Manila, was reduced by torture to a state which was described by different witnesses as 'vegetable' and 'animal'. She showed me the palms of her hands to which the electrodes had been attached. They were like nail-marks. Electrodes had also been attached to her nipples, and there had been a threat to insert them in her vagina. Her nervous system had been severely assaulted.

The 'vegetable' state was one in which it seemed impossible to get through to her. The tears would roll down her cheeks but there would not be a flicker of understanding of the world around her. She was in this state when Ed de la Torre found she had been put in the same jail, and somehow managed to get access to her. He spoke to her for a full half hour without knowing whether anything had got through at all. He suspected that she had named colleagues under torture, or had been afraid that she had done so unwittingly in that world of unreality and nightmare into which she had been thrown. So he spent the whole time assuring her of the forgiveness of God. That comes first, he kept insisting. If you have something to repent of, you can do that later. But God's love and forgiveness come out to meet and hold you where you are now. He had to go away without any sign but it looked as if this penetrated her subconscious.

When I met her some time later, she had decided not to speak of her experience to anyone, and asked her deputy to give me the story instead. But she got annoyed at the way he narrated the event and took over, giving me a vivid account in her own words.

I asked her if God remained real to her in it all? 'Nothing remained real in that nightmare world,' she replied. No relationships of any kind mattered. She had completely lost her grip on God. But just once or twice there came a break in the dark clouds. Then she knew that God was reaching down and holding her. Even though that realization was again lost in the world of unreality which engulfed her, she came through convinced of this saving thing: God kept a grip on her.

* * *

PRAYER

God the Lord

We pray for those who are tested almost beyond endurance:

– who go through such agony of bodily suffering as we have never known;

– whose spirits are shredded by pressures coming from every quarter or whose minds are reduced to a state of torpor.

God the Lord

Hear the cry of broken humanity where justice takes cover and 'the prudent keep silence in that time because it is an evil time.' (Amos 5.13) Hear the cry of broken humanity where laws are designed for the benefit of the powerful and victims have no redress. Hear the cry of broken humanity where no one can be trusted, where 'brother will deliver brother to death and a father his child; and children will rise up against their parents and have them put to death.' (Matt. 10.21)

We bless you, Lord God, that you hear cries, not just prayers. The distress of people comes to your ears as did the groaning of your people in Egypt because of their harsh taskmasters. Stretch out your hand to save.

We lift up for your healing and blessing:

– people harassed because of their race and colour, and brutally op-pressed;

– people of lowly classes and castes, despised and rejected;

– those subject to sexual assaults and demeaning practices;

– refugees from war and from cruel regimes;

– prisoners bound in affliction and iron.

Lord Christ

may people learn to look to you and find a companion in their distress:

– for you were despised and rejected, called a son of Belial;

– you were hungry and thirsty and had nowhere to lay your head;

– you were the butt of soldiers and their cruelty;

– you were lashed, tortured, and put to an agonizing death.

When people can no longer hold on to you because of the agony they experience – still, we pray, keep a grip on them.

Amen.

GUATEMALA, 1980

As I entered Guatemala City, news came through of the assassination of a priest, Fr Faustina Villanueva Villanueva. Deaths of priests made the headlines. Hundreds and thousands of Christian catechists, delegates of the Word, leaders of small ecclesial communities were being eliminated too but these went largely unreported. But it is important that the need to remove priests existed. It showed that they were with the people. For the official Church to be with the people is always a threat to repressive regimes.

Those killed need not have been particularly radical. This priest was not. But he was greatly loved by the Indians in his area, and he greatly loved them. The people in that region were terrorized. Troops would enter a village, herd the men out, rape the women, browbeat the children and take anything of value they could find in the poor houses. Nuns had had their centre raked with bullets.

The priest had been at a meal when two men called. When he enquired as to their business, one shot him through the side of the head. He fell forward and the other opened the back of his head with a close-range shot.

The floor where he had fallen forward was covered with blood. His people gathered earth sufficient to absorb the blood. The blood and earth were put in a box. They held a vigil beside it all night. The next day it was buried in front of the altar.

At the funeral four bishops and forty-seven priests were on parade. It was public affirmation to such killers that there were plenty more who stood by the faith who were ready to die if need be.

I asked, 'What is the effect on people of these murders, which are only the tip of an iceberg?' I was told, 'We are both more scared and more firm. With the example of our martyrs before us and the resurrection of Jesus Christ at the heart of our existence, we know that evil will be defeated – with or without our life.'

* * *

PRAYER

God the Lord, we recollect:

– *it is often in the face of persecution that the Church becomes truly your people standing with one another fearfully and hesitantly yet with determination because your Spirit takes hold of them and fills their weakness with strength;*

– *it is often when we are robbed of status and clout according to human standards that we can offer you our emptiness which you can fill to accomplish your work in and through us;*

– *it is often when we are at the end of our tether that we discern small ways forward, robbed by then of that stumbling block – trust in ourselves.*

Give your Church the grace not to aim at secular influence but to see you, in the worst circumstances, opening out opportunities for faithful living and witnessing.

Give me grace, however I am placed in life, to see you inviting me to accept my situation as a gift from you, however unpromising it may seem, for you can do exceeding abundantly above all that we ask or think.

We recollect also:

– *we must learn to handle power, for you put us in charge of the Creation, calling us to shape it your way;*

– *we must learn to work with those in power, for they are called to be your servants and their service is due both appreciation and criticism;*

– *we must learn the instrumentalities of power so that we may not take refuge in ideals and dreams when we should be learning techniques for the creative management of life.*

Grant your Church the grace to take your Creation seriously, bending to tasks of research, honouring technical competence; that skills may be in place where they are needed to bring the whole Creation forward on its course.

Give me the grace to recognize in all kinds of people gifts for managing the world; and give me determination to offer and enlarge my own competences, that I too may play my part.

In Jesus Christ's name
Amen.

In Rosyth, during the 1940s and 1950s, a healing group of about forty met after each Sunday evening service to pray for the sick, and visited them during the week. I did not consider myself to have healing powers but was prepared to lay on hands if the need was desperate.

One day, a woman contacted us who was facing increasing paralysis. Her doctor had warned her that she had to reckon with its spread until she was totally incapacitated.

We prayed. I laid on hands. What I found shook me. A force came through me whose source was beyond me. I was taken aback to find the rough way in which I commanded the evil to depart from a person and the very physical sense of implanting new life to replace it. It was as if I had let another power enter in to take charge of the situation. I was simply its accessory.

Later she went for a check-up. 'What's happened to you?' asked the doctor.

'You tell me.'

'I told you that what you could expect was total paralysis. I now tell you that what you can expect is to recover the use of your whole body. What brought this about?'

'You tell me, you're the doctor.'

'Well, I'm not a religious person but I think it must be the Great Healer at work.'

While visiting around the parish, I heard of a woman, not a Church member, who had cancer of the liver. I visited her, and friendship and trust grew. She had no Church connection but was glad to know of the prayers for her of the healing group.

One day she told me where she stood: 'If Jesus Christ wanted it, I could rise from this bed here and now and walk across to you, made perfectly whole. If Jesus Christ wants it, I can go down to death and be raised on the other side, made perfectly whole. I am ready for whatever healing he chooses to give me.'

* * *

Jesus once said, 'I have not found such faith, no not in Israel.'
(Luke 7.9)

REFLECTION

ILLNESS AND DISABLEMENT

Why am I set aside like this, Lord Christ?

I could be up and doing, using time entrusted to me to some advantage – to your advantage. You will ask me to account for that time at the end of my days. There is energy I could be using positively, creatively, constructively, but wherever I turn you meet me with closed doors; and it is as if you have shut them, they have not shut themselves. It is as if you want me to be set aside, useless.

Is this what Saint Paul experienced when the Holy Spirit headed him off from the provinces of Asia and Bithynia? A missionary to his fingertips, within easy reach of people who had never heard the gospel. If ever two and two needed to make four it was then. But it was as if you had a place in your plan for futility, for waiting and wondering, for finding every move frustrated. It was as if Paul had to experience emptiness and uselessness as part of the maturing of his life. Is there 'someone from Macedonia' waiting to come to me in a dream also, summoning me to new fields, if I have patience?

Or have you something better than that for me? Am I set aside in order that it may be brought home to me more clearly that the excellency of the power is of you and not of me? Your Kingdom can flourish with me on the sidelines. Do I need to learn that? I have time to absorb it now.

Or is it that, since you have given me abounding energy, you want me to realize how many of your children have constricted lives and constricted opportunities for serving you? They are set aside day after day and still they can be a praise to you. Must I become a child again that I might enter the Kingdom?

Maybe I need time to dream. Have you stopped me in my tracks, Lord Jesus, to release my imagination and set me exploring in worlds of the spirit? Or is it simply that I am now given the chance to absorb what it was like for you to spend thirty or so years tied into the routine of each day. Were you itching to get on with your mission, waiting impatiently for the signal, but held back time after time?

John Wesley prayed: 'Let me be used for thee or set aside for thee.' I know which I find the harder. But give me what is in your will for me.

Amen.

DR ARCHIE CRAIG'S DEATH

DR ARCHIE CRAIG WAS A GREAT BIBLICAL SCHOLAR
AND ONE-TIME MODERATOR OF THE CHURCH OF SCOTLAND

Margaret and I may have been the last ones outside his family to see Archie before he died. His wife May, in 'God's impeccable timing' as Archie put it, had passed away just before him on Thursday 22 August 1985. I had been asked to take the prayer of thanksgiving for her life in the service at Doune on the following Monday. Already, by Sunday, I had prepared the prayer – but it was a prayer of thanksgiving for the life of both of them, for who could separate Archie and May?

On that afternoon, Margaret and I phoned to ask if we could call in to see Archie after the Monday service. We were told that he was sleeping but would be consulted when he woke. It came to me that we would be asked to visit that same afternoon, that Archie had no intention of waiting any longer to die. We stayed near the phone. Sure enough, he woke up and asked if we were free to go across there and then. We found him awake and alert. First, with that grace which was so much a part of his nature, he thanked us for not visiting, except on odd occasions, in the last few years. Margaret and I had concluded that the amount of visitors, along with his wife's illness, was wearing him down. We made an agreement that he would take the initiative and phone us if he ever wanted any help or just a chance to talk.

Then he told us about May's death and his gratitude that she was happed away safely before him. With boyish glee he recounted her last words. First came her affirmation, 'Archie belongs to me!' (which must have been doubly satisfying in light of a distressing question she addressed to him in her confusion some time earlier: 'Does the name Archie Craig mean anything to you?') Then she asked for a prayer and the Lord's Prayer was said. She responded, 'That was lovely!' (These were also Margaret's last words after the communion service our minister, Catherine Hepburn, took at her bedside.)

We talked just a little more. Archie was satisfied that he had been able to sign off with us. As we left he composed himself to sleep, and not just to the sleep of nature. He had settled himself to sleep into the next life, where he would wake to rejoin May.

I would like to meet the atheist who, seeing Archie die, would still hold that there is nothing beyond.

* * *

'And I heard, as it were, the voice of a great multitude and as the sound of many waters and as the sound of mighty peals of thunder, saying "Hallelujah!" For the Lord our God, the Almighty reigns. Let us rejoice and be glad and give the glory to him, for the marriage of the Lamb has come and his Bride has made herself ready. And it was given to her to clothe herself in fine linen, bright and clean; the fine linen is the righteous acts of the saints.' (Revelation 19.6-8)

PRAYER

Almighty God

We stand in awe before the promise you hold out for the whole of Creation and especially for us, human folk, put in charge of it as your trustees. It is not enough that you have made us in your image. What is in store can be compared to nothing so much as a marriage in which we share your life wholly and completely – we, who are creatures becoming united with you, the uncreated. It takes our breath away. Blessing and glory and honour and power be to you for ever and ever.

We give thanks that the union is with the Lamb slain – Jesus Christ who put death in its place that it might have no more dominion over us, transforming it to serve his purposes. Now we who might be fearful of dying need no longer fear death itself any longer, praise to your holy name.

We give thanks that the Church's bridal garment is made up of the deeds of those who have sought to live your way, whose lives are made complete in your presence; both those who have known and acknowledged Christ, and those who fed the hungry and clothed the naked without at that time knowing to whom they were responding.

We give thanks for those who have helped us see life and death in true perspective, so that we neither avoid the demands of life nor the final challenge of death.

Help us so to number our days as to fight with all the saints to set up signs of your Kingdom of joy and truth, of love and peace on earth, which is your footstool; and one day to know your reign made perfect in heaven which is your throne. There unite us again with all those whom we have loved and parted from, that we may together rejoice in you eternally.

Then all glory shall be yours, for ever and ever

Amen.

There was nothing noticeably wrong with Margaret's health during the first few days when we were contributing to a consultation at Bossey, the World Council of Churches' Ecumenical Institute near Geneva. As the second half of the week began, swelling around the middle of her body and in her legs became perceptible. By Sunday 17 May, she was unable to get into any of her dresses and had to wear a pair of trousers which had an elasticated waist.

On Monday 18 May, I was wakened around 3a.m. and *told* (don't ask me how), 'You have to get Margaret home.' Before others were astir, Ofelia Ortega and her husband Daniel Montoya and I had looked at the options in the light of the deterioration in Margaret's condition. The programme was adjusted to allow our main contribution to be made in the first period next morning. Then we would catch a plane back home.

That Tuesday morning, Margaret was not fit to take part in our usual 'double act', but her eyes affirmed that what I was saying was being said for both of us. She came forward to share with me in responding to questions.

We had been warned to leave not later than 10.45a.m. since there was the journey to the airport, tickets to be got and paid for, procedures for boarding. At 10.45 I said to the company that we had been able to bid farewell to a good number so would they please understand that we had to go straight out, without more ado, to the waiting minibus? Not a bit of it! They moved in from the sides to the centre aisle. We could not take half a step without being hugged, kissed and stroked. Then the whole company, in a moving procession singing songs of the Kingdom, conveyed us to the minibus. They blessed us on our way with a quite tangible outpouring of love.

One of the participants, reflecting on it in retrospect, called the whole spontaneous action 'an event of divine choreography'. A piece of Scripture came to mind. It was the ride into Jerusalem. This time a death was very much in prospect. It took little to imagine a second procession, equally tumultuous and loving, waiting for Margaret on the other side. The cancer raged through her until, on Ascension Day 1987, her life was crowned.

* * *

Death took you kindly, and was kind to me
bereft of all your warmth and grace and love,
leaving no presence – trace where you would be,
turning me outward, making me onward move
    I knew not where.

Death took you kindly and was kind to me:
all that I hated bore a touch of grace –
life ebbing out was your being set free
your leaving us was for the Father's face
    no parting there.

Death took you kindly, left me torn in two,
grateful for life fulfilled, laid safe to rest:
but o the ache for sight, sound, touch of you,
grieving your absence, sure all's for the best,
    wrestling in prayer.

And shall I boast my faith 'Death, where's your sting?'
when one so fresh and lovely left my side?
I trust faith's unbelief to God, and cling
humbly and gratefully to one who died
    risen life to share.

After her death, Margaret featured in my dreams from time to time. In three of these she came back to let me know how it was now to be between us. One which stands out occurred on the night of 25 June 1988 when I was in Siena, Italy. I felt at the time that it was to be the last of its kind. So it has proved till now. This was the dream.

Margaret and I had been asked to meet with a Free Church congregation and share with them ways in which we had developed parish work in Rosyth in the 1950s. There had been a lively, thoughtful meeting of minds. The pleasure we had at that encounter still remains with me, so rarely did such an opportunity for dialogue at that end of the ecumenical spectrum occur.

Then I lost Margaret. I went searching for her in the grounds of an estate with fields and trees. She was nowhere to be found. I reached the crown of a grassy knoll. There she was, coming up the slope towards me. 'I have been looking for you everywhere!' I said. 'Thank you for looking for me,' she responded. 'It was just that I had such a sense of contentment that my future was in God's hands and felt such pleasure in this summer dress (actually she was wearing a blouse and shorts) that I felt I had to go away for a bit by myself just to take it in and relish it. I have done that. Now it is lovely to see you again.'

She joined me and we walked along, her shoulder nestling into mine and my hand round her body, which I could feel under the favourite summer dress which she was now wearing.

At one point she stopped, turned and held up her face. We had a long deep kiss of commitment. As we moved on, she said once more what a difference it made to have the assurance that her future was in God's hands. I knew that referred to the cancer. I felt I had to say, 'But you may not escape, you may still have to go through with it.' 'I know I may still have to go through with it,' she answered, 'It will still work out well.' We walked on, out of the dream.

It was that sense of travelling in close unity which remained with me even more than the kiss of commitment. I was assured that Margaret intended to companion me closely through the rest of my earthly life.

* * *

'I am convinced that there is nothing in death or life, in the realm of spirits or superhuman powers, in the world as it is or the world as it shall be, in the forces of the universe, in heights or depths – nothing in all creation that can separate us from the love of God in Christ Jesus our Lord.' (Romans 8.38-39)

REFLECTION

Reflect on the incredible gift of marriage – another life so intimately and joyously intertwined with one's own; and on close relationships other than in marriage – friendships and blood-ties so mutually enriching. Dwell on the incredible gift represented by Jesus Christ crucified and risen – that in him death has no more dominion. Beyond death lies not love's destruction but love's fulfilment.

Pray for those who have been left desolate by a loved one's death, feeling abandoned. May they be assured that Jesus Christ knows what it is like for them, that his cry of forsakenness on the cross testifies to solidarity with them in their bewildered grief. Looking to the same Jesus Christ, may they find what follows the cry and know that death has lost its sting; now nothing can separate us from Jesus and from those who are with him.

Pray for those to whom death brings liberation as well as loss: a loved one freed from pain and distress; a marriage or friendship which had been faithfully pursued after it had lost its savour, now thankfully ended; a life submerged by a partner, now given opportunity to flourish in its own right; a life rounded and made complete and safely folded away. May there be no guilt in the realization that death provides freedoms as well as withdraws them.

Pray for those who, when death occurs, regret bitterly their failure to have invested the thought and time and energy and affection which would have crowned the relationship and fulfilled it. May they not merely accuse themselves but seek, through confession, your forgiveness and restoration; that their lives may be even more fruitful, thus pruned.

Rejoice in the Lord always, and again I say Rejoice.

The Lion of Judah

flames out

on the desolate land

from his ambush of joy

        Ravished

        slain to life

        sing

                'Nothing, nothing,

                nothing, nothing, nothing,

                now can destroy.'